A Fish Tale
A Trade Off:
Practical Accounting Principles for Fishing Skills

RG Bud Phelps

Copyright © 2017 RG Bud Phelps

All rights reserved.

ISBN-13: 978-1535279215
ISBN-10: 1535279214

TABLE OF CONTENTS

	Foreword	5
	Supportive Letter	7
	Shared Thoughts	9
	Acknowledgements	13
	Introduction	15
1	Don's Frustration	19
2	Nebraska to Canada	23
3	Raleigh Lake – Day 1	33
4	Raleigh Lake – Day 2	39
5	Indian Lake – Day 3	59
6	Arethusa Lake – Day 4	73
7	Hawk Lake – Day 5	79
8	Heading Home	97
	Epilogue	105

RG Bud Phelps

Foreword

I have known Bud Phelps for over 5 years now. In the spring of 2011 I met Bud at the first SCORE meeting I attended. SCORE is a nation-wide organization of volunteer business mentors who help small business people and entrepreneurs by mentoring and consulting with them on issues in their business. At the meeting when I mentioned that I was from Curtis, Nebraska Bud immediately spoke up and said he was from Curtis as well and that was the start of our friendship.

I had just been let go from my job as a tax accountant at a small accounting firm in Omaha. I was miserable with my career choice and preparing income tax returns was not my cup of tea. I was desperately searching for a reason to continue with the accounting profession, (a profession that I now love and enjoy) and Bud was the answer to my prayers. Before meeting Bud I thought that all accountants and certified public accountants could do was preparing income tax returns, auditing and bookkeeping, but Bud opened my mind to a new world. Bud had such a different viewpoint. He said that accounting and accountants are there to help business people understand their business on a deep level and accounting helps business people gain knowledge and wisdom over their business lives. Accounting is not for preparing income taxes or sales taxes or for reporting their results to their bankers. It is for themselves first and foremost! Bud inspired me to break away from the traditional path of a CPA and to follow my heart. I want to thank Bud from the deepest part of myself for being there for me at a time when I needed him the most.

A Fish Tale is a great story about fishing as well as accounting and what accounting can do for you. Accounting may seem like a boring subject to read about, but accounting can be really fun and interesting when it pertains to you and your business. I have witnessed this fact many times in my consulting career. When a businessperson can relate their accounting to their business and goals, when they use it to help them achieve their goals, they love it. They actually say "this is exciting", "this is interesting and meaningful", "I feel so much better" and so on. The point is you have to customize your accounting to fit you and your business in order to make it real for you. Bud emphasizes this point many times in this book.

Bud also makes it exciting to go on a fishing trip to Canada and the lodge and lake mentioned in this story is a real place. I want to go catch some "lakers" and "northerns" sometime soon and now I may have some idea of how to do that. This is also a wonderful tale of friendship that I hope I can tell someday.

I hope this book starts you on a journey. A journey to discover accounting and what accounting can do for you. I urge you to delve more into the accounting of your business and to become more proactive with your accountant, with your bookkeeper and your business life.

Enjoy the story!

Kelvin M. Kemp, Certified Public Accountant

Supportive Letter

A Letter from Brooke R. Lenhoff, Assistant Director, Southeast Community College Entrepreneurship Center

I have had the privilege of knowing Bud for about 10 years. I was just starting out in my career when I first met him, and I immediately knew he was special. Anyone who meets him can see the enthusiasm he has for helping others in their business journey. His face lights up when he talks about the people he meets in his time teaching workshops for the Southeast Community College Continuing Education Center and as a former volunteer SCORE mentor. Bud has always encouraged me to push myself in my career and has treated me as his equal despite the decades of experience and wisdom he has on me. He is a true example of a lifelong learner, mentor, and a friend.

It was after an All In Startup book club event I hosted at the SCC Entrepreneurship Center that Bud told me his idea for this book. I was intrigued by the idea because knowing Bud, I knew it would be fantastic. I also thought he was a little crazy because I had no idea how anyone could turn accounting principles into a fictional story, much less a story about fishing! I was shocked (and amazed) when he showed up in my office less than a few weeks later with his first draft, then later his second, and then later his seventh!

I know that he is beyond excited to share this information with you through this story, and I hope that you can feel his passion and enthusiasm cheering you on as you read it!

Brooke René Lenhoff
Assistant Director
Entrepreneurship Center
Southeast Community College
Lincoln, Nebraska

Shared Thoughts

Several of my pre-publishing readers have shared their thoughts about this book, **A Fish Tale,** and I am passing them on to you. Please share your own thoughts through the review process on Amazon or by posting them on my Facebook pages, https://www.facebook.com/budsbooks.

Mike Groenewold

I enjoyed Bud's book, **A Fish Tale**, since it partially recreated a recent trip we took to his favorite lakes in Western Ontario, Canada. For Bud the trip served as a homecoming of sorts, to Cobblestone Lodge, where he annually visited and fished at surrounding lakes with friends for 30 years. For me, his son-in-law, the trip was a new adventure, having never fished in Ontario. The Fishing adventures that Bud weaved between accounting lessons, illustrated the great times he has enjoyed with old friends and me at this special place.

As a Horticulturist, I knew very little about accounting practices. But after reading his book, I now have a basic understanding of methods to track both income and expenditures. And as well, I learned that certain techniques can be used to determine the equity of a company at any point in time. Also, I now know that security checks can be established to protect a business owner's investment.

I highly recommend, **A Fish Tale**, for entertainment and practical accounting advice.

~~~

Bob Matoush

I was very interested in the new book by Bud Phelps, A Fish Tale, which combines a fictional story about a fishing trip and teaching a friend on the trip about accounting principles. Being an avid fisherman myself, the narrative about the fishing trip was very interesting to me and brought back great memories of trips of my own and the excitement of catching a fish no matter what size, but the bigger the catch the better the story is.

The way Bud combined the accounting principles with fishing intrigued me because of my cost accounting background at Goodyear. I was perhaps a little skeptical how he was going to integrate the two in the beginning. But, the way for someone needing to know some of the very basic account structures, Bud made following the natural flow of accounts very easy to follow with a simplistic road map.

So, I would recommend this book as being both entertaining and informative.

Randy Arnold

Senior Vice President for a large Banking Firm for the last 35 years, has worked in a number of accounting roles and recognizes the importance of accurate recordkeeping and the story that proper accounting tells Senior Managers and business auditors. He shares the following about Bud's book. ***A Fish Tale***, blends the excitement of a fishing trip and the basic principles of Accounting into a story line that peaks your interest and lures you in.

Bud's excitement to learn and teach what he has spent his life doing, results in a valuable teaching tool for the classroom, which I recommend as entertaining and informative.

~~~

David Scheffler

I taught and coached for 16 years, and was involved in crop insurance from 1983 until November 2012. I trained crop adjusters and agents regarding crop insurance and am still doing this today.

I agree with Randy that Bud's book, **A Fish Tale**, blends the excitement of a fishing trip along with the basic principles of Accounting into a story line that lures you in through his fishing experiences and peaks your interest into a better understanding of Accounting.

I recommend this book as both entertaining and educational.

~~~

Ted Simonson

I must admit when I started to read, **A Fish Tale**, I thought, how can this work? But it does work, the accounting and the fishing do go together. In fact quite well. The fishing story is very interesting and the accounting lessons are presented well too. All in all I thought Bud blended the two very smoothly.

I also recommend this book as being both entertaining and informative.

RG Bud Phelps

Acknowledgments

A Fish Tale has been a brand new writing adventure for me, authoring a business book with a fictional storyline. Therefore, I have utilized a brand new approach before uploading the final draft to my publisher. I sent the template of A Fish Tale to friends and associates for a pre-publishing read. I wanted to test the readers market, through this pre-publishing read, seeing if this fictional storyline accounting book would be more acceptable than a regular test book style accounting book.

I want to give full recognition to **Diana Kander** who triggered my desire to utilize this approach after reading her book, **"all in startup"** which used a fictional storyline to explain the best approach for launching a new idea when everything is on the line. Also, even though in the middle of an important project she took the time to encourage me through emails while I was in the process of editing my book. She shared the fact that her pre-publishing readers helped her so much toward the development of her very successful New York Times Bestseller, **"all in startup."**

I selected various individuals to be my pre-publishing readers and am pleased with the responses I've had. I have included the written responses in the **Shared Thoughts** section and include the following individuals: **Kelvin Kemp-CPA, Brooke Lenhoff-Assistant Director of the Southeast Community College Entrepreneurship Center,** my son-in-law **Mike Groenewold,** Several Cornhusker Kiwanis Friends **(Bob Matoush, Randy Arnold, Dave Scheffler, Ted Simonson)**, as well as very positive verbal responses from many others.

I want to thank all of you, pre-publishing readers, for your input and suggested changes that have molded this into one of my very best business books, your support has made it possible. So, since the main purpose in my pre-publishing reader approach was to determine if my fictional storyline accounting book would generate more interest than a regular test book style accounting book. I feel the responses were very positive, and have told me loud and clear that even though they didn't really like accounting they found themselves actually understanding where I was coming from.

I want to give special recognition to my wife, **Pat Phelps**, who diligently edited each new version of, *A Fish Tale*, with the final number being somewhere over seven (counting the ones with just minor edits). Pat would always say, after she gave the edited copies back to me, ***"Now remember, my changes are just suggestions and if you feel they change your intended meaning, don't use them."*** More times than not, the changes were necessary and I can count on one hand the ones that I modified a bit rather than accepting the change.

Introduction

After reading the book **"all in start-up" - Launching a New Idea When Everything Is On The Line, by Diana Kander**, I was so turned on with her fictional storyline style I couldn't wait to utilize this same style explaining Key Principles of Practical Accounting. Principles a manager should know to properly manage their business.

Too many times I have met individuals who are so involved with their own products or services, they absolutely dislike anything to do with accounting. They either assign someone else to do it, or send all the data gathered through some accounting software program, to their local accountant for review and statement preparation. In most cases these individuals will wait for their accountant to tell them what's going on in their business (after the fact).

An accounting professor once told me that these individuals treat their Financial Statements like "Stump Reports." He called them "Stump Reports" because they are initially followed by the manager while the accountant is reviewing and explaining to them what happened the past year. But then, the statements are put in a drawer or a file and not referred to again, until next year. If you are having your Financial Statements read to you or are reading them after the New Year has already started, you'll find it a bit difficult to change the results because, that's already history...

There are Key Principles of Practical Accounting that will assist a manager throughout the year in order to keep them up to speed as to what is happening in their business, both positive and negative. Don't have your "Stump Reports" stuck away in some file or drawer. Allow these Practical Accounting Principles to become your Business Floatation Device like your Personal USCG Fishing Vest.

Principle#1 – Chart of Accounts

This total listing of accounts is developed to create the accounting paths necessary to provide Financial Statements meaningful to your specific business. Why not develop accounts that do create accounting paths relative to your specific business?

Principle #2 – Financial Statements

Financial Statements are the economic history reports developed from all of the economic transactions. (Examples: purchases for cash or on account, and sales for cash or on account).

Principle #3 – Management Footprints

These are developed over a period of time through the study of your business' Financial Statements and therefore will flag important items you should be watching.

Principle #4 – Internal Controls

Internal Controls are established for the management of procedures that provide protection of the company's financial assets and employees.

You can find all kinds of accounting books on line, just Google accounting books, and you'll see what I mean. I promise you my accounting book will give you the keys toward a better understanding of Practical Accounting through a fun fishing experience. You may know your products or services very well, but not how the economic history of your company is revealed. Utilizing the Practical Accounting Principles presented here can really help you become a more knowledgeable and wiser manager.

This book, *A Fish Tale* – **A Trade Off: Practical Accounting Principles For Fishing Skills**, by RG Bud Phelps, will bring out these principles throughout a fictional sharing process, hopefully in a way that will help individuals gain the fact that accounting is really not a swear word…

This story begins with me going on a fishing trip many years ago when I first met Don Seeman. Don, at the time, had worked for a filtration manufacturer in Minneapolis, but had already started his own company doing basically the same thing, filtration manufacturing and service.

This fictional story will show me, sharing Practical Accounting Principles with Don, as a trade-off for his expertise in fishing skills. I will learn new Fishing Skills during the day, and teach Don Practical Accounting Skills after dinner. Don had already started his new business but was frustrated with his in-ability to understand accounting. Don admits that he didn't follow his Financial Statements during the year. Therefore, he was frustrated when he received his reports from his accountant and it was too late to make changes that will affect last year's operation. That was already history…

An Accountant is *expressing* what the Bookkeeper *recorded* during a given accounting period in order for a business person to react in real time to changes in businesses, allowing a more *proactive* action for the financial condition of their business.

Too many times I have been called in as a consultant when the owner is so frustrated with his lack of accounting skills. I have been in the accounting field, mainly working within an industry, rather than being a CPA preparing annual reports and tax returns.

Being an accountant for several small manufacturing businesses has given me a deeper understanding of the need managers have to understand how the financial history of a company is written.

There are many self-help books about understanding accounting, but I haven't seen one that relates to the Practical Accounting Principles through a fictional storyline. Please contact me through a review of this book on Amazon or through my web site if you have found this to be a positive experience…

http://budspracticalaccounting.com/contact/

1 Don's Frustration

Tom Benson lives in Plymouth, a suburb of Minneapolis, and has been buying our swimming pool supplies for his customers in Minnesota. Tom was visiting me in Lincoln when he shared the frustration a young friend, Don Seeman, was having because of his lack of understanding basic accounting skills.

"Bud, with your accounting background and knowledge, I think you could really help Don. He started his own company a couple years ago and is frustrated with his lack of accounting skills. I would like to invite you to join me and my small fishing crew, "Canadian Fishing Crew" (CFC), this spring fishing in Western Ontario. I know Don has great fishing skills plus he's a good cook. He could teach you his Fishing Skills and you could teach him Accounting Skills."

"Thanks Tom, I really would like to experience Canadian fishing and would be glad to have a 'Trade Off' with Don, Fishing Skills traded for Accounting Skills."

Tom called to tell me that our new "Canadian Fishing Crew" (CFC) is all set for this spring. I would drive to Plymouth, a suburb of Minneapolis, and Don's brother John would drive to Plymouth from Marshall, MN and spend the night at Don's house. The "CFC" would leave from Tom's early the next morning. Usually we will stop somewhere along the way to buy our provisions for the week, or Tom may want to visit the local Walmart instead. Tom gave me a suggested list of the things I should bring along for the trip to Canada. Tom suggested I bring the following list of things I would need, but not to "overdo it," because there would be four of us in his vehicle…

The list included both regular clothing and foul weather clothing, two spinning rods and reels strung with fresh 12# test monofilament line, my tackle box with an assortment of spinners and spoons, a stringer, a small first aid kit, a backpack to carry the items I want with me on the boat, and of course my "US Coast Guard approved" Fishing Vest (lifesaving flotation device). I did add two things; a waterproof pouch for my camera and a case for my spinning rods.

Preparation for the fishing trip to Canada is similar to what I go through before teaching my Practical Accounting class at Southeast Community College. I have developed my Practical Accounting Class Packet through many years of experience in the field. I always include in the packet the following information for my students: copies of my PowerPoint and all of the related handouts. My accounting class packet is my student's lifeline, similar to the "USCG" fishing vest flotation device which is the fisherman's lifeline in the deep lakes of Canada. I'm totally comfortable with what I have prepared for my class because of my many years in Practical Accounting, but my lack of experience makes me wonder if I've prepared properly for this fishing trip.

My next Practical Accounting class is just over a week before I head for Minneapolis. I have been able to isolate four basic Accounting Principles for my students: (1) Chart of Accounts, (2) Financial Statements, (3) Management Footprints, and (4) Internal Controls. Once my students "get it," it's like you can see a light bulb go on over their head. I need to find some simple methods for teaching Don the principles of practical accounting as a "Trade Off" – Accounting Skills from me and Fishing Skills from Don.

A Fish Tale

All of the gear I've gathered for my trip hasn't given me the answers or confidence I feel is needed to be a good fisherman in the Canadian lakes. Proper preparation is necessary and vital for gaining the most out of either; fishing in Canada or understanding the key principles of accounting. My fishing experiences in Nebraska just haven't given me the same confidence in my skills I have gained over the years in the field of accounting.

I love the outdoors, and the Canadian lakes are beautiful, so why is it so hard for me to relax and get into the swing of trolling for Walleye, Northern, or Lake Trout. Knowing what rigs to use and when you should change and try something else? Knowing how long you let the fish suck on your minnow before giving them that little flip, that results in a hooked fish, and how different species of fish strike your rig setup. Knowing why you need to change rigs when you're fishing for different species of fish, and what are all the different rigs you can use. Why does the color of a spinner make any difference and when should you change to another color? I would love to know some Fishing Principles so that I can be as comfortable fishing as I am in understanding and utilizing Practical Accounting Principles!

Hey, relax, now you're even talking to yourself about this.

~~~

Don called Tom again, sharing his additional frustration with his new company, Britewater, which showed a loss for the year. He was seriously thinking about cancelling out on this Canadian Trip but his brother John and Tom pitched in to pay for his share of the Cobblestone Lodge charges.

They both told him he needed to have this time to refresh his thinking about "Britewater" and to learn some accounting principles from me, on this Canadian fishing trip. Principles that will make it easier for him to understand how the economic data is recorded on the company's books, and how he can read that information throughout the year, from his accounting reports, so that problems can be nipped in the bud earlier.

I asked Tom for Don's phone number so I could talk to him before the trip.

I called Don and advised him about the "Trade Off" of Accounting Skills for Fishing Skills; asking him to bring me some basic information about his company. He told me that he would bring the Chart of Accounts the accountant had given him but wanted me to know that he really didn't understand where his accountant was coming from. Again, he was frustrated with his lack of understanding.

I could feel the frustration in his voice!

2 Nebraska to Canada

Lincoln to Plymouth (a suburb of Minneapolis) is 440 miles and I will have my car all gassed up and loaded with everything I'm taking along for the trip for an early morning start. My weather check was good, predicting a bright clear spring day for the trip all the way up through Minneapolis so it should be an uneventful trip.

As planned, I got away from our place by 7:00 am, with a stop in Ames, IA for an early lunch and to top off the gas. It was a smooth trip and so I was pulling into Tom's place in Plymouth right at 4:00 pm in the afternoon. Tom had taken the afternoon off and was watching for me, he was walking out to greet me when I drove in his driveway. I noticed that his garage door was open and his Wagoneer was parked behind their Buick. He motioned for me to pull in on the side of the driveway leading to the empty stall. I parked and jumped out for our traditional hug.

Tom exclaimed, "It's great to see you my friend! Your timing is good as usual, you must have had clear sailing."

"Well Tom, the weather was perfect and I really didn't run into too many road repair situations."

"Bud, we'll transfer your stuff to the Wagoneer except for what you need tonight. It will save us time messing with it in the morning, and you can just pull your car into the garage."

"Great Tom that will be nice to have my car protected while we are gone."

We transferred my duffel bag, rods case, tackle box, and backpack to his Jeep, taking my small overnight bag in with my stuff for the night. Tom led the way into his home, and as we entered Tom called for his wife, Elva, to come on down to greet me.

Elva came in the entryway with a smile on her face. "Bud, it's so good to see you again. Come on in and make yourself comfortable. Tom will take you up to the guest room and I'll fix us a pot of tea, if you like."

"It's good to see you again too Elva, and a cup of tea sounds fantastic. I've been at it since 7:00 am this morning and I'm a bit road weary."

"I bet you are Bud. Tom, why don't you guys go on up and I'll get the tea started."

Tom and Elva's home was really well done, nestled in a nice grove of trees, and decorated well. Tom took me up to their guest room which I had used on a previous business visit, and said to come down to the kitchen when I finished. I was familiar with the room and where the guest bathroom was located, so I washed up a bit and went down to their kitchen. Elva had everything ready and added a small plate of homemade cookies for us to enjoy with our tea.

After our tea and cookies, Tom suggested we go to Walmart here and pick up the groceries rather than stopping on the way. He called Don and invited him to join us at Walmart around 5:30 pm with his brother John.

~~~

We drove to a Walmart that was relatively close to Tom's home and waited in the entrance area for Don and his brother. They arrived at 5:30 pm and Tom made the introductions. I immediately liked both Don and his brother John, but thinking to myself, 'Don sure looks young to be a fishing expert.' Shopping didn't really take us too long because Tom had made two lists, one for himself and one for Don. We set out in different directions and I just followed Tom around the store picking up what he told me to.

We finished shopping and were discussing what to do next when Tom suggested we go out for dinner with Don, his wife Judy and Brother John. Don liked the idea and suggested a lounge they both were familiar with. Tom told me he had already talked to Elva earlier about the six of us going out for dinner and she liked the lounge that Don had mentioned. We went back to Tom's place and put the groceries in the back of his Wagoneer; putting the things that needed to keep cool in Tom's large cooler.

We all arrived about the same time at the lounge, so as we were walking in Don introduced me to Judy, and Elva to his brother John. We had a great dinner, a couple glasses of wine, and very enjoyable company. We didn't really rush things along, but I was glad when Tom suggested we call it an early night.

Since Don lived in Plymouth, Tom had told him we would just swing by his home on the way. It's approximately 425 miles from Minneapolis to Cobblestone Lodge so Tom wanted to get an early start. We would be stopping somewhere along the way for lunch with our goal being to drive into the Raleigh Lake Road around 4:00 pm.

Tom would be taking US35 toward Duluth, and the short cut at Cloquet toward highway (53) going to International Falls. After reaching International Falls we would cross over the border into Fort Francis, Canada. From Fort Francis we would travel East to Atikokan, and then North to Western Ontario's highway 17, then East to Raleigh Lake Road.

Northern Minnesota has beautiful country to drive through and we have been taking turns driving as it's a long stretch for one driver. Luckily this gave me a chance to get acquainted with Don while we sat in the back seat, with Tom and John in the front. Don was telling me about his frustration with his business venture and had brought along everything his accountant had given him! Hopefully I could help him understand accounting for his business in exchange for him helping me with his fishing expertise. It sounded like a good tradeoff to me…

Don wanted to utilize his years of experience in building and servicing filtration tanks and Diatomaceous Earth Filter systems. He had worked in all areas in the company and was well respected for his skills. After so many years working for someone else, he wanted to open his own company which would build and service water filtration equipment, with the city of Minneapolis and surrounding suburbs being his target market. My first question to Don was, "Did you develop a Business Plan for your business?"

"I planned on writing a Business Plan but really haven't started to develop it yet. The closest to it was to register my company name as 'Britewater,' which is a play on the fact that our equipment will be making water clean and clear."

Don added, "However I'm not sure what the best way there is to develop my Business Plan."

"Well Don, I've read many books on the development of Business Plans and would suggest you buy the book **'all in startup'** with the subtitle, **'launching a new idea when everything is on the line.'** This is the best business book I've read about things you should know and do before starting a new business. Plus it's written with a fictional storyline."

"Wow! That's the kind of business book I could handle. I'll check it out when we get back from our trip."

"Also, I would like to go over some basic Practical Accounting Principles you should consider for your company. Having a Practical Accounting System that utilizes these key principles will give you the basics toward understanding your company's Financial Statements. I can review these principles with you on this trip. In exchange you can teach me some key Fishing Principles that will make me a better fisherman both in Canada and back home."

"Bud, you've got a deal! I'm not an accounting fan and would really rather spend my time perfecting my 'Britewater' offering for my customers."

"I understand Don, we all like to concentrate on the skills that we feel comfortable doing."

We were talking about a multitude of general things for the next couple of hours and finally Tom called for a lunch break at Minnesota's "Famous Halfway Stop" in Hinckley, Tobies Restaurant and Bakery.

We had a delightful lunch at Tobies and Tom's *selection was* outstanding with their own bakery items. Our normal male comradery featured earlier Canadian fishing experiences shared by Tom, John, and Don...

Tom told us he had fished with another group for years but for unknown reasons the group broke up. Don also fished with a younger group of guys and enjoyed the fishing part of their trips more than their comradery. He felt they had completely different interests and was just glad to have the opportunity to fish with Tom and his brother again. Lunch was over, the car was all gassed up, and we were back on the road again for our last leg of the trip. As we continued our trip to Cobblestone Don shared information about his favorite three lakes in the area; Arethusa Lake, Indian Lake, and Raleigh Lake.

Arethusa, he felt, was one of the best Walleye lakes while Indian provides both great Walleye fishing and some big Northern Pikes. He said the lake where Cobblestone Lodge is located, Raleigh Lake, is one of the best Lake Trout lakes he has ever found, and that Raleigh is actually three lakes connected. You might know, the best one is the 3rd lake which of course is the farthest away from the lodge.

I was impressed with Don's sharing and Tom was probably totally correct in assessing Don's fishing skills. You could just feel it when he was telling about his experiences on those three lakes. This is going to be perfect. Don seems so willing to share his fishing skills but obviously needs help in understanding accounting. It's a slam dunk and I couldn't have set it up more perfectly...

A Fish Tale

Don will share his fishing skills and I'll share my accounting skills so we both will benefit. I really need to walk through the Practical Accounting Principles very carefully and non-clinical. I'll utilize a "good old boy" approach so as not to scare him off or have him shut down because he's bored. Accounting can be boring if you let it…

We were now in the Northern portion of Minnesota where the pine groves become more plentiful and the homes fewer and fewer. Beautiful country, but I bet it would be a challenge up here in the winter!

We arrived in International Falls and Tom quickly got in the line where we would cross over into Canada. The line was several blocks long; consisting of cars, SUV's, and pickups with a large percentage of them towing boats. Right here is where the excitement builds!

Tom said, "Okay guys, this is how it's going to be. When we reach the window, where you see everyone stopping, we will be asked several questions about how long we are going to be in Canada and where we will be staying. Next your ID (Passport), the amount of 'booze,' the cartons of cigarettes, and the food you're bringing into Canada. Follow my lead, and only answer the questions asked, don't add anything, and be totally polite! The Border Patrol doesn't appreciate smart-alecky remarks. I've seen them pull a group over and have them unload their vehicle and boat on the tables provided, just because of what someone said. This is really serious business for them, as it is their responsibility to protect Canada by making sure everyone entering answers the key questions correctly! "

The line seemed to inch along as the Border Patrol went through their questions but finally, it was our turn. Tom answered the questions exactly as he had advised us.

When it came to the food question Tom answered that the amount of food was just what we would need during our stay in Canada (their question was to assure them we weren't bringing food in to sell).

We all went through the questions and finally with a smile on the Border Patrol person's face, we were allowed into Canada. We passed quickly through Fort Francis and were on our final leg to Cobblestone Lodge! Having been advised earlier that our cabins would be ready for us after 3:00 pm so we were right on schedule as it would be closer to the planned 4:00 pm arrival. We only had a couple of hours left on the road and by this point in time, everyone was suffering a bit of TB (tired butt).

We pulled off of the highway and followed a road that took us by Raleigh Falls, then across a bridge spanning the river coming out of Raleigh Lake. Finally up the little hill, and there was our destination, Cobblestone Lodge. Tom pulled up in front of the lodge and we all got out and stretched. He led us up the steps to the lodge office and Denise met us at the check-in counter. She is the co-owner of Cobblestone Lodge along with her husband Cliff, and they both welcomed us for a week of Canadian fishing! Cliff and Denise were very friendly, pleasing us with their genuine hospitality. While each of us were checking in, Cliff explained the gas program for the boats, what we would need in each boat when we took them out on the lakes, and how they were scheduled.

A Fish Tale

We lucked out with the only two log cabins left with Don and I taking the smaller one, with Tom and John right next door. Tom and John's cabin was just a bit larger with a good sized dining table, so all of the cooking and eating will be in their cabin.

We unloaded all of our gear, parked the Wagoneer next to the two cabins, and prepared each for our week's stay. I was pleased to be bunking with Don as we will be able to spend some quality time sharing each other's skills in the evenings. Just below our two cabins was a small beach. Cliff had built a cinderblock area for camp fires in the evening as well as a grill for everyone to use. Tom said his previous group had spent several evenings down there drinking a few beers, singing, and even roasting some marshmallows! Both cabins had small decks where we could put our coolers, tackle boxes, and fishing rods. Each deck had a couple chairs so we could sit outside and enjoy Raleigh Lake in the evenings. Tom gave us a shout on his way by, and asked us to join him at the main lodge as soon as we got through setting up our cabin.

It had been a long trip but having a new friend made the time pass by quickly. Don and I are all moved in and have everything setup for the week. I love this old log cabin! These two log cabins are the last of the originals which were built back in the 30's. Sometime in the past, a fire took out the original lodge and four of the original log cabins. So we are the lucky ones! Looking out on Raleigh Lake I was struck immediately with the beauty of the scenery. Don and I had gone out on our deck and were just enjoying the view when we heard our first loon, evidently calling to his mate! Talk about setting the scene, you couldn't ask for anything more perfect!

Don said, "I hate to break up this relaxing moment, but we should head for the lodge and see what Tom has on his mind, I bet he wants to go out on Raleigh this afternoon."

"That would be great Don! I'm sure ready to test our skills at fishing Lake Trout."

"I'll show you some tricks of the trade, Bud."

3 Raleigh Lake – Day 1

Since it was still relatively early Tom had asked Cliff if we could take a couple boats out on Raleigh Lake, and Cliff said he still had two available. Tom suggested I fish with Don so we could get better acquainted. I thought to myself, 'it's so neat how a plan can come together like this.' I would be able to start my Fishing Skills training right away!

Don was totally familiar with picking up a full tank of gas from the supply next to the pump, and hooking it up in the boat we were going to be using. I carried my rods and backpack down to the boat and also loaded Don's gear while he was hooking up the gas to the motor. Tom and John were doing the same and quickly we shoved the boats off of their racks and were ready to head out.

Tom suggested we try "The Willows" in a small bay in the 1st lake because he had been successful there in the past. He would have preferred going all the way to the 3rd lake, but today it's "The Willows" because of our late start. Tom led the way and Don followed for the short trip. We arrived at a small bay with a shore line populated with a grove of White Birch trees, which had been nicknamed "The Willows."

Tom swung their boat around into the small bay near the Willows and stopped while we set up our rigs. Don stopped just behind their boat and started with his instructions about how he fishes for Lake Trout.

First he showed me how to remove the double hook from the "strip-on" and thread the short wire through the mouth of the minnow.

He then showed me how to place the double hook around the body of the minnow saying that this was definitely a tried and true method of saving minnows and catching Trout. Next he showed me how he will allow his line to drop down behind the boat as we did our slow troll alongside "The Willows" beach.

He told me not to put my line out but to just watch his action during this first run. I payed close attention how, when his line went tight, he would allow the line to go out by moving his rod tip slowly toward the back of the boat. Finally, I saw the line jump slightly as the Trout was starting to suck on the minnow. Don showed his patience by allowing the Trout to pull his line back, and it seemed at the right moment, he flipped the tip quickly to set the hook as he felt the tugs on the line. He kept pressure on the line while reeling in our first Lake Trout toward the boat. Don asked me to get ready to net the fish as soon as it got close enough to the boat. While I was netting the Trout I saw Tom bringing one in toward their boat.

We stopped at the far end of the beach and watched John net Tom's Trout. Don said, "Bud, you've just had your **first Fishing Lesson** of this trip so you owe me one. We'll call this one **'Patience Pays'** and I'll explain. The advantage of the **'strip-on'** lure is that a Lake Trout is an expert in sucking off minnows. Threading the wire through the minnow with that double hook snugly around the minnow, makes it next to impossible for the Trout to suck it off your **'strip on.'** When you first feel the Laker pulling on the line, you patiently give him some more line by letting your rod tip point toward the back of the boat. When you do feel the fish pulling back on the line, and usually you may feel the fish jerk it just a bit."

"Now, when that happens just flip the tip of your rod forward quickly, and you'll know by the feel that you have him hooked. Like I said, don't hurry it, your reward is a Laker for dinner."

We swung back around to make the next run. This time I would have my opportunity to try out this first lesson. I took the double hook off of the strip on and threaded the wire through the minnow, making sure the double hook was snug around it. As Don started the run I let out my line as was shown to me and quickly felt a fish making a slight tug on my line. I played it out, and after a couple quick tugs on my line I flipped the tip as Don had shown me and maintained pressure while reeling it in.

I was trying to duplicate Don by maintaining pressure on the line as I was reeling in the fish. I kept bringing the Trout toward the boat and noticed that Don was already waiting with the net. When Don plucked that fish out of the water I experienced the thrill that comes when you have completed a task by following instructions given to you! We fished at the "The Willows" for a couple hours with our boat bringing in four Lakers and Tom's boat bringing in three. I was completely thrilled with our first day of fishing and would chalk this up to a great learning experience. Now, more than ever, I felt committed to help Don gain an understanding of "Practical Accounting Principles" for his business venture.

We headed back to the cove where Cobblestone was located and I was surprised how quick the trip back went for us. I think it was because I was still on a high from having Don's "Fishing Skills" lessons work so well for me. We docked our boats and took our fish to the screened in fish cleaning station Cliff had provided.

Cleaning Lakers is relatively an easy process when you're planning on grilling them. Don suggested that I just observe how they cleaned the fish as another skill to add. All three of my fishing partners made quick work of cleaning the Lake Trout leaving the head and skin on as they planned on grilling them for dinner. We left the boats tied up as we were scheduled to be on Raleigh again tomorrow.

Don was true to his statement regarding our reward. He grilled the Lake Trout in foil after covering them in Olive Oil with a bit of Oregano shaken on top. What a great topper for our arrival day; Lake Trout, a glass of wine, along with scrumptious sides, including beans and hash browns! After dinner Don and I headed for our cabin.

We decided to take advantage of the beautiful evening by enjoying one more glass of wine out on our deck before starting our accounting lessons. We were both still pretty charged up but I wanted to start my pay back this evening with my first Practical Accounting lesson for Don. We added a cup of hot tea for each of us and I suggested the starter for this evening would be the first **Practical Accounting Principle.**

Principle#1 – Chart of Accounts

I didn't want to get too far out in the weeds of accounting as it had been a long day, full of lots of excitement.

"Don, the Chart of Accounts you brought me, is the total listing of your accounts and should be edited to create the accounting paths necessary to provide Financial Statements meaningful to your specific business. I suggest we re-structure your Chart of Accounts for better accounting paths."

Don said, "I wasn't involved in setting up any of these accounts. My accountant did that for me but didn't explain what it meant."

"Well Don, tonight I want you to understand what is meant by an 'Account' and the listing of them. I brought along this notebook to record interesting things on this trip, but would rather you used it to jot down notes about these Practical Accounting Principles."

I continued, "An Account, as used in accounting, can best be defined as a 'named item' used to record each financial transaction that takes place during an operational period. The underlying reason an Account is so important is that they will give you a logical place to record your accounting transactions in a certain way. This will give you the understandable *pathways for developing the economic history of your company*. The 'Chart of Accounts' that your accountant prepared for you is a typical listing of all of your accounts, but I don't feel they track your company's history in a way helpful for you."

"I feel that it's important for us to edit your current Chart of Accounts in such a way as to *improve your economic history pathways*. I want you to participate with me in this improvement of your Chart of Accounts. By doing so you will have a much better understanding of the economic operations of your business. You can select key accounts you want to glean information from and they'll be positioned accordingly when you create your Financial Statements."

"Wow! Bud, my accountant just told me he took care of this listing to give me information he thought I would need."

"I can see that most of the accounts he selected for you are really common but you should know what they are there for. We can go over his listing and I'll explain the accounts as we go along. We can add numbers to the accounts also."

"Do we have to add numbers to the accounts Bud?"

"No, but I find the numbers help in the placement of the accounts on the Financial Statements (reports) of a company."

"I didn't bring the reports that he made for me at the end of this last year."

"That's okay, I'll show you how they'll look while we're working on your Chart of Accounts. Why don't you just keep your Chart of Accounts you brought from your accountant with that journal I just gave you? That way you can make notes in your journal about the individual pieces of information you brought along."

"This is great Bud, now I'll be able to ask questions about all these sheets without feeling like a dummy."

"You're not a dummy Don, unfortunately your accountant took too much for granted, thinking you had a better understanding than you did. But, before we get too far into this, let's stop at this point. I don't want to scare you with too many things in our first session, and since it's so late let's call it a night."

"Good point Bud, I want to be able to understand each step and already have a lot of questions, so let's do hit the sack!"

4 Raleigh Lake – Day 2

Morning came with the bright sun shining into the cabin and me hearing Don hustling around in the kitchen. He saw I was awake and said, "The coffee pot is on and I'm going to take a quick shower. You can brush your teeth at the kitchen sink, have a cup of coffee, and I'll be out shortly."

By the time I had brushed my teeth and was just starting to enjoy my cup of coffee, Don popped out of the bathroom. I quickly finished my coffee and jumped in the shower.

Don yelled "I'm going on over to Tom and John's cabin. I'll see if I can help get breakfast started and you can come on over when you're finished."

Our first full day had officially started and as I walked over to Tom and John's cabin I marveled at how beautiful the lake looked and how blessed we were with such a gorgeous clear, blue, sky.

The wonderful smell of bacon and potatoes frying caused a bit of a stomach growl as I reached the top step. Opening the door I saw the table all set; Don and John were bringing the breakfast over to the tables heaped up on two platters. Tom was already sitting at the table drinking a cup of coffee, probably not his first. I sat across from Tom with Don and John on both sides of me. Everything tasted wonderful and now I understand where Tom was coming from. Don and John are great cooks!

Tom suggested we pack a lunch of sandwiches, munchies, some fruit, and a cooler full of bottled water. Everyone agreed with the lunch menu; just enough to keep us on the lake for the day.

We all pitched in to wash the dishes and put the cabin back in order after our great breakfast. Last evening we had tied up the two boats at the dock closest to our cabins so we didn't have far to carry everything we needed for the day, except for the gas.

Don suggested we go to the 3rd lake, getting the longest trip on Raleigh out of the way early. We could always work our way back through the 2nd lake and maybe even ending up where we were last evening, at "The Willows." We would stop at the dock next to the gas pump to pick up fresh tanks of gas for the longer day.

Cliff met us over at the gas pump with fresh minnows and his guide tips regarding which spots the Trout were hitting best. Tom and Don both were familiar with the spots mentioned and asked about a couple of other locations. Cliff's directions were to troll along the rock wall down to the corner were the river comes in, then circle back out into the bay, then repeating the same pattern in front of the rock wall. The other spot is the point just before the Rock Wall bay.

Off we went for the long boat ride over to 3rd lake. We safely passed through the short connecting channels into 2nd and 3rd lakes and made our way to the other end of 3rd lake.

We would be passing by the only cabin on Raleigh, called Americans Camp, owned by a lawyer from Chicago. They had to bring everything necessary to build this beautiful little cabin by boat. Cliff had told us that he has known the family that owned Americans Camp ever since he bought Cobblestone and they were always very pleasant. Tom said that he had fished in their small bay catching several Lakers at a lunch stop.

A Fish Tale

Arriving at the point that reaches out in the lake we stopped to get our rigs ready for our first run of the day. Don handed me a minnow and I started threading it on the strip-on, replacing the double hook snugly around the minnow. I had at least remembered that part of Don's lesson!

Don said, "Are you ready for our first run?"

"I sure am, Don!"

Tom and John had already started their run and Don fell in not too far behind them. Making sure he left enough room for Tom and John to let out their lines behind the boat.

I was tense! I felt the line slipping back out behind the boat, and when I had reached enough line I was ready for some action. Don felt the tug of a Trout first and started the game of letting it have more line. At that same moment, I felt the tug on my line and let my rod tip point toward the back of the boat. I felt a stronger tug and flipped the tip toward the front of the boat, feeling that I had planted the hook and had a Trout on my line! Don saw what was happening and said, "Keep your line tight we could have our first double of the day! I'll bring mine in first. I'm just about to the boat, and can net it myself. Then when you bring yours in I'll net it for you."

"Okay Don, I really have a fighter here but I'm gaining and he'll be nearing the boat shortly."

Don netted his Trout just laying the fish in the bottom of the boat while he came over to my side. His timing was perfect. My Trout was very near the boat so he dipped the net and brought it in!

Don shouted to Tom, "We have our first double of the day!"

All I could say was, "Wow, lesson learned!"

"You did good Bud, no panic, just a steady hand like you're supposed to."

I was pleased and could tell that Don was too. We looked over and saw Tom netting a Trout for John. He yelled over to us, "Good going guys, you're ahead of us because I missed mine."

We made one more run with no hits. Tom suggested we go over to the Rock Wall and come back here, if nothing happens over there. We followed Tom around the point and made ready for our first run along the rock wall.

Don said, "We'll start this run as soon as we pass the point you see ahead of us. Then follow the shore line in front of the rock wall toward the place you can see the river coming into the lake, then circle back out into the bay, back to the point, and do the same thing all over again. Be ready, especially when we pass the rock wall. We have always had at least one hit right there!"

"Here we go again Don, this is great!"

We had just passed the wall when Don got a hit. I watched him hook the fish and start the process of reeling it toward the boat. I was able to net Don's fish still maintaining pressure on my line. Don had told me that sometimes you needed to let out a little more line to get some spinner action on your rig, so I gave it a try. As the line went tight I felt a slight tug so I gently pointed the tip toward the back. The fish hit hard and I flipped the tip hooking him and maintaining the pressure, reeled him in toward the boat.

Don netted another fish for me and that made two apiece for us so far. I saw that both Tom and John had caught fish on this same run. It was one of those rare times that you have an opportunity to be on such a high note where everyone is on the same page. Smiles were shared all around as both Tom and Don allowed the boats to come along side each other. We all stood for a huge sharing of high fives for the eight Trout we had in the boats! The two boats gently rocking as we looked out across Raleigh and just soaked it all in!

Tom said, "Guys, this is one of those rare times when everything comes together and all of our fishing skills, long owned or just learned, resulted in a perfect run."

I couldn't hold back, "Don, thank you for the simple clues you gave me that enabled this to happen. I was doing the things you taught me as if your hands were on my rod guiding me, and it felt so right!"

"Bud, you are a natural. I watched you on that last run and everything I had suggested for you to do, happened. Way to go! I enjoyed every moment of it as much as you did."

Tom added, "Don's right Bud, you weren't just going through the motions – you were showing us a natural. My compliments to you as being a good listener. Way to go!"

John joined the accolades but pointing at his younger brother he said, "Don, you certainly brought Bud into the category of a Trout fisherman who has just gained the touch we have all looked for. Way to go Don! We have all enjoyed these runs, and let's go back to our cabins so we can celebrate with a couple of beers while we enjoy our lunch."

Three cheers echoed off of the Rock Wall and we turned our boats back to Cobblestone for a special celebration. Even though the distance was the same, it seemed like our boats had gained new found speeds as we made our way back for a special sharing time over lunch in our cabins. Cliff saw us pull in to the dock nearest our cabins and came down to see if something was the matter and said, "What goes guys? I thought you were out for the day."

Tom explained, "Well Cliff, something special just happened at 3rd lake with our friend Bud coming into his own as a Trout fisherman. We decided to celebrate with a couple beers while we enjoyed a special lunch in our cabin."

"Great to hear guys, you just do that and then get back out there and catch some more Trout! It sounds like we now have four Trout fishermen in our midst."

I actually blushed like a young high schooler that had just met a new girl, when Cliff included me in that category. Wow! Cliff offered to clean our eight Lakers while we were eating lunch, and brought them up to us just as we were finishing. He hesitated a minute and coming back in the cabin he said, "I've been thinking since our conversation earlier about our new Trout fisherman, Bud, and I'd like to offer something special for you guys. I would like to take you out in my Whaler to a very deep part of 3rd lake and give him the experience of fishing for the bigger Trout, utilizing downriggers. Downriggers have manual winches with a cannonball type weight to carry your fishing lines and lures down to a specific depth. By utilizing my downriggers you'll be fishing at the 60' level where the big boys feed.

"I have two downriggers so two can fish at the same time and then trade off so all four of you will have a turn. My guests have found it to be both exciting and profitable."

"Some have caught Lake Trout that weighed up to 20 pounds! The record for a Raleigh Lake Trout is closer to 40 pounds. I have a couple rods set up with steel leaders, silver, gold, or fluorescent spoons and heavier line to allow you to catch the big ones."

I looked around the room and found that I wasn't the only one with his mouth open! "Cliff, I am honored that you would offer to guide us for this special search for the bigger Trout!"

"Bud, I have a bit of a selfish motive. I know that when you guys experience this you will be back up here for years to come, and this is just a good way for me to promote Raleigh Lake and Cobblestone Lodge. Plus, I like you guys, you're my kind of fishermen."

We didn't need our rods or tackle boxes as Cliff was supplying everything we needed. After the four of us had taken our seats Cliff cruised out of the bay heading toward the opening to 2nd lake. We reached the opening and were heading through 2nd lake at a much quicker pace and before you knew it, we were passing into 3rd lake and following the same track we had been over this morning. Then Cliff turned into another bay before we reached the Rock Wall, heading toward the middle of the bay. Cliff said, "Okay guys, I'm going to start with Tom, being the oldest, and Bud being the newbie as the first two to utilize the downriggers. You two take your seats by the downriggers and I'll help set them up for you."

Cliff snapped the downriggers to our lines, after allowing 20 yards of line to flow back similar to how it would be if we were going through a shallow troll. Next he lowered our lines off of our reels down to the 60' level as shown on the downrigger's line counter. He started forward at about the same speed that we had been going at the surface level. Cliff said, "Okay guys. When a Trout hits your lure the connection to the downrigger will release and you will feel him tugging on your line. Maintain your pressure on the line and reel your Trout in with steady even turns of your reel. You'll know it's a bigger fish by the feel and he will be twisting every which way to get off your line!"

It seemed that both of us had a fish on at about the same time! I was watching what Tom was doing and trying my best to duplicate his efforts. I could definitely tell I had a bigger fish on my line by the way he kept twisting back and forth on the way in! Cliff was standing right behind me with the net at ready and Don was standing behind Tom doing the same. My trout broke the surface just behind the boat so I tried my best to keep a steady pace reeling him alongside the boat!

"I got him!" exclaimed Cliff as he dipped my Trout out of the water.

"I got Tom's too!" yelled Don as he dipped Tom's into the boat.

I couldn't believe it. I knew my eyes were as wide as they ever had been! "How much do you think it weighs Cliff?"

"Bud, it has to be at least a 10 pounder!"

"Wow, that's so neat, I can't believe I was able to do it."

"Like the guys said earlier, Bud, you are now an official Trout fisherman and have added a 10 pounder to your reward package."

"How big is yours Tom?"

"Well I can't really say for sure Bud, but if Cliff says yours is a 10 pounder I think I caught his twin!"

Excitedly, Don and John were patting us on the back and highfiving us, then telling us to get out of the way so they could have their turn! Once Don and John got all rigged up, Cliff again started the troll speed. After the first swinging turn both of their lines snapped lose and we had two more fish on! Once these two fish were in the boat it looked like we just drew four of a kind! This was an afternoon I wouldn't soon forget and my debt of sharing Practical Accounting Principles had just risen another notch.

Soon after our downrigger experience, Cliff quickly made the trip back to Cobblestone Lodge, telling us that he would clean these trophy fish as he wanted us to take these four home as perfect as was possible. We immediately put them in freezer paper with our names and cabin numbers written boldly on the packages! What a day! I know I can't claim to be an expert Lake Trout fisherman yet, but I'm a lot closer than I was two days ago!

Don and John had gone back a bit earlier so they could start our Trout dinner with all the trimmings. We went back to the cabins after watching Cliff clean our fish, leaving our floating minnow buckets tied to the dock closest to our cabins in order to save as many as we could for tomorrow.

When we opened the door to Tom and John's cabin the wonderful aroma of fish, fried potatoes, and beans did cause our stomachs to growl a bit!

Tom opened a bottle of sweet red wine and poured four glasses for us to enjoy before dinner. Don had told us to relax and enjoy the wine, as it would be a little longer before everything was ready.

I made a toast to the group, "All right gentlemen, I want to take this opportunity to thank you for the fishing skill lessons you have taught me these first two days by offering this first toast of the evening."

The responses from the three were spontaneous, "Here, Here, Here!"

We enjoyed another wonderful dinner, cleaned up the dishes, and put Tom and John's cabin back in order. Don and I excused ourselves and went back to our cabin.

The timing was perfect! We had stopped fishing early because of the successes we had on the 3rd lake. I was glad because it would give me more time to share Practical Accounting Principles with Don…

We would be going to Indian Lake tomorrow. Cliff had reserved two of his boats up there for us. Tom asked him about what spinner rigs the Walleye were hitting on, and what spots on Indian have seemed to be the best at this time of the year. Cliff is such a great lodge owner, and his goals are to make our experiences here the most enjoyable ones…

Tom was familiar with the spots Cliff shared and told me his success had always been positive at those spots. The first spot was a long beach with a reed bed just off the shore located just before you went through a shallow passageway into the next section of Indian Lake. That was Don's favorite spot on Indian.

When we got settled down and were having our cup of tea I said to Don, "I've been thinking about giving you a different approach while explaining these Practical Accounting Principles. I'm not teaching a student seeking a grade for an accounting course, but a friend needing a practical accounting process."

"I told you the first night that your 'Chart of Accounts' is a listing of all of the accounts used in recording your company's historical financial transactions. And the fact that we are working toward the improvement of your Chart of Accounts will give you a much better understanding of the economic operations of your business. This is all true, but… what does all that accounting speak really mean? First let's relate the accounts to individual items in your tackle box which are there for specific reasons. As an example… your strip-on rig is in your tackle box as a special rig for catching Lake Trout. The account titled Cash in Bank-Checking is in your Chart of Accounts to show the additions and subtractions from your checking account over a measured period of time."

"In fact, every single 'Account' in your 'Chart of Accounts' is there to accumulate historical financial information over a measured period of time. Your reports will show these account balances in the same position on them every time, giving you the keys for managing your company."

I could see that Don was struggling with that concept and said, "You mean to tell me that my listing of accounts can tell me what has transpired historically over any period, or at the end of any period of time?"

"No Don, the reports tell you that! First I'll show you the reason for putting the 'Accounts' in certain groups as you want them to appear on different reports explaining your businesses financial history. Each 'Chart of Accounts' will always start with the 'Accounts' that will appear on a report called the Balance Sheet. The named ***Accounts*** on the Balance Sheet (report) will either be an ***Assets*** (something the company owns), a ***Liabilities*** (something the company owes), or ***Equity*** (the ownership investment accounts)."

"Don, I'm going to show you several groups as they appear on your company's Balance Sheet, and we will write them down in your notebook for future reference or expansion. This listing of 'Accounts' will hopefully 'turn on the light bulb' of understanding as to why they are listed in this manner. You will see this listing of 'Accounts' as they will appear on your report called the Balance Sheet, and you'll better understand why they are listed in this manner."

"Okay Don… let's look at the ***Balance Sheet*** named accounts, on the listing your accountant gave you. This may sound strange Don, but by following my directions and editing the accounts on your listing exactly as I read them off, will allow you to picture them just as they will appear on the Balance Sheet. Every Balance Sheet that you'll see from this point forward will be in this exact format. We'll be utilizing a four number system both for simplicity and to leave room for expansion."

A Fish Tale

Balance Sheet – Key Accounts

- Current Assets
    - 1000 – Cash on Hand & In Bank
        - 1010 – Cash in Bank – Checking
        - 1020 – Cash in Bank – Savings
        - 1030 – Petty Cash – On Hand
    - 1100 – Accounts Receivable
        - 1110 – Accounts Receivable – Customers
        - 1120 – Accounts Receivable - Others
    - 1200 – Inventory
        - 1210 – Inventory – Raw Material
        - 1220 – Inventory – Work In Process
        - 1230 – Inventory – Finished Goods
    - 1300 – Notes Receivable (short term)
        - 1310 – Notes Receivable - Other
    - 1400 – Prepaid Items
        - 1410 – Prepaid Insurance
        - 1420 – Prepaid Advertising & Promotion
        - 1430 – Prepaid – Dues & Subscriptions
- Fixed Assets & Other Assets
    - 1500 – Fixed Assets
        - 1510 – Buildings
            - 1515 – Accum Depr – Buildings
        - 1520 – Production Equipment
            - 1525 – Accum Depr – Prod Equip
        - 1530 – Office Equipment
            - 1535 – Accum Depr – Office Equip
    - 1600 – Other Assets
        - 1610 – Organization Expense
            - 1615 – Accum Amort – Org Expenses

Current Liabilities
    2000 – Accounts Payable
        2010 – Accounts Payable – Vendors
        2020 – Accounts Payable - Other
    2100 – Notes Payable (short term)
        2110 – Notes Payable – Bank (ST)
        2120 – Notes Payable - Other
    2200 – Taxes Payable
        2210 – FICA Taxes Payable
        2220 – Federal W/H Taxes Payable
        2230 – State W/H Taxes Payable
        2240 – Federal Unemploy Taxes Pay
        2250 – State Unemploy Taxes Pay
    2300 – Accrual Accounts
        2310 – Health Insurance Payable
Long term Liabilities
    2400 – Notes Payable (long term)
        2410 – Notes Payable - Bank
Equity
    3000 – Equity
    3100 – Owner's Investment
    3200 – Retained Earnings

"Don, see how easy it is to define the grouping on your Balance Sheet accounts as we have done, you can quickly look at the individual groups to see where the action is going on with your assets and liabilities. You will see how many dollars of Current Assets you have to pay your Current Liabilities with. This Current Ratio rule of thumb is, a company should have $2 in Current Assets for every $1 of Current Liabilities."

A Fish Tale

"Whoa Bud… remember I don't know any of this stuff. Show me what you mean?"

"Okay Don, The Balance Sheet is a snap-shot of the company's Assets, Liabilities, and Owner's Equity at a particular point in time, and will be different the very next day."

"Now I want to show you an example of a section of the Balance Sheet that details the Current Assets and Current Liabilities. I am using your accounts as we have edited them with the new account numbers and putting them into their proper position. I'm also using example dollar amounts, allowing us to compute the company's Current Raito. Managers have the ability to compute the company's Current Ratio each time a Balance Sheet is prepared."

"As I said before, and it's worth repeating; The Balance Sheet is a snap-shot of the company's Assets, Liabilities, and Owner's Equity at a particular point in time, and will be different the very next day. Usually the Balance Sheet is prepared monthly, quarterly, or annually. It is always a good idea to compare the current Balance Sheet to one prepared at the same point in time in each previous period. This comparison makes it easier to see changes that have happened in the new period."

~~~

"Please note that I am just using the following Balance Sheet grouping to show you how Current Ratios are computed. Your true Balance Sheet will show the exact numbers at the date the Balance Sheet was prepared."

Balance Sheet (Example for Current Ratio)
Current Assets & Current Liabilities
December 31, 1976

Current Assets
1000 Cash	$ 55,000	
1100 Accounts Receivable	$ 65,000	
1200 Inventory	$ 125,000	
1300 Notes Receivable (ST)	$ 35,000	
1400 Prepaid Items	$ 20,000	
Total Current Assets		$300,000

Current Liabilities
2000 Accounts Payable	$ 65,000	
2100 Notes Payable (ST)	$ 55,000	
2200 Taxes Payable	$ 10,000	
2300 Accrual Accounts	$ 20,000	
Total Current Liabilities		$150,000

"Don, looking at the Balance Sheet (Example), which covers these two groups, you will see that $150,000 in Current Liabilities divided into $300,000 in Current Assets will give you the 2 to 1 Current Ratio. The Current Ration Rule of Thumb is $2 in Current Assets for every $1 in Current Liabilities."

"Wow! That's pretty neat Bud! Do you mean to tell me that I can compute their Current Ratio on each Balance Sheet Report my accountant has given me?"

"Yes, Don, individuals' use their Balance Sheet Reports as management tools and purposely compute this Current Ratio to monitor their liquidity. Liquidity… is a measurement looked for by bankers."

"Now Bud, that makes perfect sense! Thanks for showing me that feature, it was a great way of cementing the basic idea regarding what the Balance Sheet is all about!"

"Don… The following is the *Income Statement* accounts with Control Account number grouping."

    4000 – Income
        4010 – Water Filtration Tanks
        4020 – Diatomaceous Earth Filters
        4100 – Water Treatment Service

    5000 – Cost of Goods
        5010 – Water Filtration Tanks COG
        5020 – Diatomaceous Earth Filters COG
        5100 – Water Treatment Service COG

Operating Expenses
    6000 – Operating Expenses
        6010 – Operating Salaries
            6011 – Payroll Taxes
        6020 – Utilities
            6021 – Electricity
            6022 – Gas
            6023 – Water
            6024 – Cable & Website
        6030 – Insurance – Contents
        6040 – Operating Supplies
        6050 – Equipment Rentals
        6060 – Equipment Repairs & Maintenance

Selling Expenses
- 7000 – Selling Expenses
    - 7010 – Salesmen's Salaries
        - 7011 – Payroll Taxes Sales
    - 7020 – Advertising
        - 7021 – Media
        - 7022 – Promotion
        - 7023 – Printing
    - 7030 – Trip & Show Expenses
        - 7031 – Lodging
        - 7032 – Travel
        - 7033 – Food & Entertainment
    - 7040 – Sales Supplies

Administrative Expenses
- 8000 – Administrative Expenses
    - 8010 – Officers' Salaries
        - 8015 – Payroll Taxes Officers'
    - 8020 – Office Salaries
        - 8025 – Payroll Taxes Office
    - 8030 – Office Supplies
    - 8040 – Insurance – General Liability
    - 8050 – Computer Software
    - 8060 – Office Equipment Repair
    - 8070 – Interest
    - 8080 – Bank Charges
- 9000 – Other Expenses
    - 9010 – Federal Income Taxes
    - 9020 – State Income Taxes
    - 9030 – Miscellaneous Expenses

"Now, do you see where I'm coming from Don?"

"You know Bud, 'the light bulb is beginning to come on', it may still be a bit dim but I'm beginning to have a better understanding and can see where you're going with this. I know I'll have questions, but it's starting to make sense. Also, that breakdown of the Income Statement groups, really is meaningful to me. I can see how quickly you could latch on to the group information as a perfect guide. Especially when you have the control accounts to show what's going on within each group of Income and Expenses."

"That's great Don! We'll be reviewing all of this before you actually put it into practice, so don't worry about it. My goal for this session was threefold:

(1) To give you a better understanding of what is meant by an account, and a Chart of Accounts.

(2) To show you how a company can compute their Current Ratio utilizing the Current Assets and Current Liabilities section of the Balance Sheet, divide Current Liabilities into Current Assets.

(3) To show you how the account groups show up clearly as Balance Sheet accounts or Income Statement accounts. Also how this grouping is giving you a better understanding of your reports and the activities of your accounts during or at the end of a period.

~~~

"We have covered a ton of stuff tonight Don, but by having it written down in your journal it will be much easier for you to do your review. Let's call it a night as I am ready to learn some more fishing skills tomorrow."

"Bud, you're getting me hooked, so to speak, on this accounting stuff. Thanks for laying it out in a way that I can both understand it at the time and have the information available to review later."

5 Indian Lake – Day 3

I heard Don stirring around in the kitchen and knew I needed to get with it. We were faced with a long day. We'll be traveling to and from Indian Lake over original logging roads, and spending a lot of boat time getting to the spots Cliff had told us about. Same routine… Don made the coffee, jumped in shower while I enjoyed my first cup. He would pop out of the shower, quickly dress, and head over to Tom and John's cabin to help with breakfast. I noticed it was much earlier than usual but understood the reason… Indian Lake was a much larger lake and it took longer to arrive at each spot.

By the time I arrived at Tom & John's cabin the same aroma was floating in the air, the aroma of 'guy's type' of breakfast. There was no dilly-dallying today… we quickly ate breakfast, cleaned up the dishes, and were ready to roll to Indian Lake.

We picked up our minnow buckets, and met Cliff over by the Fish Cleaning Hut to dip out the dead ones and add the new. Don and Tom were getting the gas tanks picked up while John and I were putting our equipment in Tom's Wagoneer. Everything came together rapidly as our team was really clicking this morning, and before you knew it we were heading to Ignace.

We drove through Ignace, taking the main highway north on the edge of town. We were only on this nice paved road for a couple of miles when we turned off on to the old logging road taking us to Indian Lake. Fortunately Tom and Don had been there before…

I did see a small sign saying Little Indian just before we got to the side road with an arrow pointing toward a partially hidden opening. Tom backed the Wagoneer down to the short trail leading to the boats and everybody did their part in carrying all of the gear, gas tanks, and lunch cooler for our day's adventure on Indian.

We shoved the boats off the racks and made our way across Little Indian passing through the Agimac River channel leading into Indian Lake. When we left the river and came out into Indian Lake Tom and Don pointed our boats toward the North for a ride seeming longer than the one to the 3rd lake on Raleigh. Again, we were blessed with a clear day and the scenery was absolutely gorgeous! Finally… I could see a long stretch of a beach and an opening into another part of Indian Lake. Tom stopped his boat near the opening, after swinging it around toward the beach shore line. Don followed suit and I could see that this meant rig time, as Tom, Don, and John were already attaching the spinner rigs to their lines. I noticed a short steel leader had been put on the line ahead of the spinner rig and so I asked Don about it.

He explained… "Sorry Bud, I was so engrossed in what I was doing I forgot to show you the Fishing Skills necessary for Walleye fishing. As you can see, I put on a short steel leader, the ¼ Oz swivel weight, and then attaching the spinner rig to it. The reason for this added precaution is twofold. First… Walleye do have teeth and when caught, have a tendency to both flip and bite with the results being lost rigs as they cut the line. Second… Northern Pike are predators, swimming around areas where Walleye feed.

A Fish Tale

The Northern Pike have sharp teeth and attack the bait from the side, sometimes cutting the line. The steel leader gives us protection for either scenario and have enabled us to not only save our rigs, but catch the fish that bites on our baited spinner rig."

"Wow! Good to know information Don, thank you."

"You're welcome. Now… you hook the minnow through the head and out the belly, making it more secure on the spinner rig. With Walleye we do a super slow troll as you will see."

Tom had already started his first run along the beach and out toward the reed bed. Don waited a bit to give Tom and John room to let out their lines.

"Bud… you can follow my lead and don't need to set idle through this run. Let out enough line to keep you far enough behind the boat and away from the props water action. Next…you maintain pressure on your line, similar as we were doing for the Lake Trout. Walleyes hit with a quicker snap at the minnow on the spinner rig, and when it does you'll quickly snap the rod tip toward the front of the boat. Don't jerk it, just have a firm movement forward to plant the hook in the side of the Walleye's mouth. You must keep your rod tip up as you firmly reel in the fish. Now we'll watch each other's action and be ready to net the first fish caught. Doubles we'll handle the same way, but I'll try to net mine first and then yours."

"What about the Northerns?"

"Bud, let me tell you. You'll know when your rig is hit by a Northern. Sometimes it feels like you snagged a log, except when it's pulling away from you. Other times, you'll feel the Northern hit and your line with it zinging out away from you. The big ones feel like they could tow your boat!"

"Same rule, keep your rod tip up, maintain line pressure, steady reeling the line. When it's in the boat take care, his jaws clampdown like a vice. Warning… retrieve the hook with a forceps tool, not your hands!"

Just as Don finished telling about the Northern Pikes I got a hit on my rig, but as I pulled my rod forward he was gone.

Don said, "I was watching, and you jerked the rod tip a tad too soon. You have to make sure that it isn't just 'nudging' the minnow. You'll do fine, it just takes time to get used to their different attack on the minnow."

Just then, Don pulled his rod forward like he was really planting it. Sure enough, it appeared that he had a fish on!

"Fish on Bud! Reel in and get the net ready, this baby feels like it has a little weight!"

I reluctantly reeled in, as of course you want to keep fishing, and readied the net for Don's fish. Don was right, his fish was really putting up a good fight and had just surfaced at the back of the boat. It was getting close for me to net. I scooped the fish up! It was a real nice Walleye, looking like it would be in the mid 20 inch range.

"Good job Don, you caught a beauty!"

"I know Bud, isn't it a nice one! I'll measure and weigh it later, but for now we'll just put it on our stringer so we can get back at it."

Looking out ahead of us I saw the net come out, and it looked like John had the net so it must have been Tom's catch.

Don put on a fresh minnow, and I had checked mine so we were ready to start another run. We were nearing the center of the reed bed and Don warned me, "Don't get spooked when the hook jumped, if it briefly snagged on a reed. It is kind-of a pain but that's where the Walleye like to feed so you just put up with it and you'd quickly learn the difference between a quickie snag and a true hit."

I had a nice hit, swung my rod tip forward quickly, and had a fish on it. I kept my rod tip up like Don had told me, keeping pressure on the line while reeling the fish in. Don noticed and reeled in so he could net my fish. I know my eyes got big when the Walleye broke the surface because he looked like a twin of Don's fish.

Don netted my fish and said, "Good job Bud, I think you matched my fish. Looks like a twin in length and weight, but we will see later. I'll go ahead and put it on the stringer for you."

"Thanks Don that was a fun happening!"

~~~

By noon all of us had reached the halfway point for our limit which is three of our six Walleye limit. So far none of us had caught a Northern, but it wasn't a surprise to Don or Tom. They both felt we would be catching some this afternoon as the day changes.

We moved our boats back down the lake a ways because Tom had noticed this big flat rock he had used as a lunch spot in the past. Don suggested we clean four of the fish for a shore lunch, and the big flat rock we passed on the way in would make an ideal spot. We tied our boats around the corner of the big rock and unloaded Don's Coleman stove and cooking supplies. Tom and John offered to clean the fish... so I helped Don set up everything for cooking.

Don asked me to open a can of the beans and put them in a sauce pan he had brought along. He started his stove, put flour with some salt and pepper on a paper plate, and had cracked a couple eggs into a bowl for dipping. He showed me how he would dip the Walleye filets in the eggs and roll them in the flour before putting them into the bubbly hot oil for cooking. Tom and John brought him the rest of the Walleye filets to start frying and it appeared the beans were about ready.

Three of us got our plates ready, with a piece of buttered bread, some beans, and finally a stop at Don's skillet for some fresh Walleye. After we were served Don put the fire under the skillet on low, filled his plate with Walleye, beans, and a piece of bread. He joined us on a nice log someone had dragged out on the rock for the same purpose.

A Fish Tale

I said, "Guys, it can't get any better than this. A great looking day, a beautiful lake, and this special rock to enjoy our shore lunch on!"

There were three responses said in unison, "Yes, Yes, and Yes!"

~~~

We decided to go on through the shallow channel opening into the other part of Indian Lake for our afternoon fishing. We could always come back to this shore line if we didn't have any luck off of the points around the threatening large rocks. Since the opening was very shallow and it was necessary to raise the motor a bit to clear the bottom. Once we got through this short shallow area the dark water appeared, showing us we were in deep water again.

Tom cruised over to the point Cliff told us about, staying far enough off of it to give us time to get our rigs ready. We had been using fluorescent spinner rigs this morning and Tom suggested we now switch to gold and silver rigs for this afternoon. So, everyone switched out their fluorescent rigs to gold and silver. Don suggested our boat start with the silver spinners with Tom and John starting with the gold spinners. This way we could switch to the one that was the most active, if necessary.

Don and I went on the near side of the point back along the shoreline while Tom and John tried the far side of the point following that shoreline. We would be covering all bases and in this way could always join the boat having the most hits.

I got a hard strike and at first thought I was hung-up on one of the big rocks or a log. When it started to pull away I thought differently. This must be one of those bigger Northern Pikes that Don was talking about! "Don, I think a Northern hit my rig and it's really pulling away from me and taking out a lot of line."

"Your probably right Bud, it sure sounds like what a Northern would do! Keep your rod tip up and start to reel back as much as you can. Make sure you maintain pressure on the line while reeling it in!"

"I think I'm finally gaining Don, but this fish is completely different then the Walleye. It keeps diving and trying to pull away! I seem to gain a little bit and then it dives and pulls out more line. What usually happens in situations like this?"

"Well Bud, it's a back and forth battle until you finally wear him out. Your only chance in keeping him on the line is by holding your rod tip up and steadily keep reeling in as much as you can. As long as you keep the fish hooked and maintain the pressure on the line you shouldn't lose him."

"Thanks for the encouragement Don, I do think I'm gaining. Just in this last couple of minutes I have been reeling more in then he is taking out, and just now I have been able to reel in consistently."

"Keep up the good work, Bud! I have the net ready and I'm sure you'll get him up to the boat shortly. There he is, just immediately behind the boat and moving in fast! Keep reeling and I'll pluck him out of the water as soon as he's close enough. I got him Bud, and he's a big one!"

"Wow! Thanks Don, I can't believe I was able to do that! How long is he? How much do you think he'll weigh?"

"He looks to be over 30 inches long and could weigh between 10 to 15 pounds. Wow is right Bud! You handled everything well, and I couldn't have done any better."

"That was really a hoot Don! You were so right! I thought I had snagged on a log until he started pulling away from me!"

We had better luck with the Walleyes over at the reed bed so decided to go back over there. We fished until 4:00 when all of us brought our limit of Walleyes back to the full limit, while Tom and I each caught a Northern. The trip back down Indian was a happy one with smiles all around... It was a very good day of fishing on Indian and our crew was all smiles!

~~~

We got back to Cobblestone in good time and it wasn't super late when we finished our Walleye dinner with the necessary fried potatoes and baked beans. So, after cleaning up and enjoying a second glass of wine Don and I headed for our cabin.

I suggested we just sit out on our deck for a bit and have a cup of tea to settle us down after an eventful and exciting day. I was still pumped about my Northern and Don was totally pleased with the big Walleyes all four of us caught so we chalked it up as a great day fishing! While we were relaxing I felt that instead of getting in too deep with the Accounting Principles, I would use this time for review.

I wanted to review the Chart of Accounts and then start more of a connection to *Principle #2 – Financial Statements*.

"Don, why don't you bring your notebook out here and we'll review where we are with the Chart of Accounts. Tonight I'd like to start the connection of the Chart of Accounts to the Financial Statements, just a fancy name for the month, quarter, or annual reports."

Don went in the cabin and brought out his notebook, opening it to the pages where we listed the Chart of Accounts grouping of the Key Accounts.

"Okay Don… the first report we will discuss tonight is the **Balance Sheet**.

Remember, this report is a snap-shot of the company:
    Assets   (items the company owns)
    Liabilities (debt the company owes)
    Equity (how much the owners have put in or accumulated).

"So, when you're looking at the **Balance Sheet** report:

> The first page will show you all of your Assets, both the ones that will turn into Cash in one year *(Current)* and Assets you have purchased that can be depreciated over its life *(Fixed and Other)*.
>
> The second page will show you all of your Liabilities, which ones are due within a year *(Current)* and the ones that will be paid off over a longer period *(Long Term)*, and finally your ownership dollars *(Equity)*."

"I think I understand this one pretty well, and I can really picture how it will look on a report. It's cool that you can see these groups on a report; with their totals showing up in the same basic position every time. This makes perfect sense to me as I'll be able to see what 'Accounts' will turn into Cash within a year and what bills I have to pay within a year. This will also tell me if I'm going to have any money left over to pay long term debt, taxes, or a special bonus for myself."

"That's right Don, and you'll be able see all of the Fixed Assets you own along with their book value at the date of the report. Plus, you'll be able to see what your Long Term debt is and what your true percentage of ownership is compared to what the portion your Creditors own. Also, it's good to know what your Equity percentage is, compared to Total Assets."

~~~

"Okay… now let's look at the *Income Statement* report. You will be able to see each group highlighted by a main number. When you are look at the report you will see group totals as big **Footprints**. Examples: The total of the *4000 accounts* will give you the *Total Income*. The total of the *5000 accounts* will give you the *Total Cost of Goods*."

"So?"

"So, if you budget your operation on being able to have a Net Profit and maintain your Cost of Goods at 60%, Gross Profit will be 40%, it's important. So, if you can see the relationship of a single Income account to a single Cost of Goods account, you'll know if it's contributing its share. Example…

If Income 'Account' number **4010-Water Filtration Tanks = $100,000** less the Cost of Goods 'Account' **5010-Water Filtration Tanks COG = $60,000**, so **Water Filtration Tanks** have a **Gross Profit of $40,000 or 40%** and truly carried its weight. Does this make sense?"

"Wow Bud, that's cool. You answered my, 'so' question."

"Now Don, carrying your Income Statement report a little further. Did you notice that I have three different group of Expenses?"

"Yes, I do. Operating Expenses, Selling Expenses, and Administrative Expenses."

"Okay... Wouldn't it be nice to know what portion of your expenses happen every day when you open your doors for business?"

"Yes!"

"Well... **Operating Expenses** are the 'Accounts' related to the daily operational costs of your business. Salaries, Heat, Lights, Property Taxes, Etc. Every day when you open the doors these costs go on no matter what happens with your sales. Don't you think it would be nice to know what this is costing your company?"

"Yes!"

"Okay... Your **Selling Expenses** are the 'Accounts' related to promoting your company through Media Advertising, Brochures, Sales Salaries, Etc. You can't pay for these promotional costs if you don't have a profit."

"Don't you think it would be nice to know how much you've spent on promotional costs so far this year, so you could cut back if you are over budget?"

"Yes!"

"Now… The same thing goes for all of the **_Administrative Expenses_** necessary to run your office including your Office and Officer Wages. Don't you feel you should be able to control these costs?

"Yes! 'The light bulb' just went on Bud! Having this kind of breakdown of my expenses definitely helps me manage my company."

"Yes, that's exactly my point, and that's the reason for your Chart of Accounts and Financial Statements… Your reports! We have edited your Chart of Accounts to the point that you will be able to follow what has happened to the accounts in your two major Financial Statements, the Balance Sheet and the Income Statement. As I told you earlier, the accounting transactions are posted to the various accounts as the financial history of your company is being recorded."

"Wow! When you explain it that way Bud, I'm really upset that I didn't understand this earlier. By me being able to monitor what is happening in an accounting period I can actually adjust my expenses when I see that they have gone over my budgeted amounts."

"Don the light bulb is shining brightly over your head and you are definitely getting it. I need to be able to show you all of this with the actual financial history of your company."

"Yes Bud, and I will want you to come back up to Plymouth to make sure I'm getting all of this started properly."

"We can certainly make that happen Don, and it would be my pleasure to help you analyze what really has happened to your company by a complete review of the reports and the individual accounts."

6 Arethusa lake – Day 4

We were up and at-um early because Cliff had two boats ready for us on Arethusa and both Tom and Don said it was a great lake for both Walleye and Northern. Arethusa is a 45 minute drive from the lodge with a good share of it over a gravel road originally built by the loggers' years ago. Cliff said he was up there a couple days ago and the road wasn't too bad and the two boats were relatively new, this being the first season for them. Breakfast and clean-up went fast as we all pitched in.

We loaded all our gear in Tom's Wagoneer along with our two gas tanks and four dozen minnows. Cliff fills the bag that we carry the minnows in with compressed air to keep them fresh for the longer trip to Arethusa. Tom drove down Hwy 17 to Ignace following the same basic way we went to Indian Lake, but then would continue on North to Arethusa. Once you passed Indian you couldn't drive this road very fast because of the ruts and curves, plus the necessity to watch for washouts as this would be considered a low maintenance road.

Finally we came to the opening into Arethusa and Tom backed in toward the trail to the boats. Fortunately the boats were close and therefore, we didn't have to carry our gear too far. Arethusa looked to be another beautiful Lake. Don was telling me he remembered two great spots for Walleye and a bay where we could catch some big Northerns. This time, Don led the way as he told Tom he wanted to try a real active Walleye spot he remembered between two islands. The two islands were straight ahead of us toward the end of this first part of Arethusa. We passed the first island and Don stopped to tell Tom his plan.

Tom brought his boat in tight to ours, and we held the two together while Don explained how he had worked this channel last time he was up here. "Tom, last year when we were up here I went past both islands and trolled along the shore lines between the mainland and the island. Then we would pass around the top of that island and fish the channel between the two islands. There are some real active points in both channels and we had strikes in both areas."

"Yah, I fished in this same area a couple years ago and we caught some nice Walleye on both runs. Why don't you and Bud lead the way and we'll stay back a bit and follow you through the channels."

"Sounds good Tom, and if they're not hitting there's a beach just beyond that long channel just South of here. When we fished that beach shore line we spotted an Eagle nest not far from the beach. I always felt that they may have built their nest there because of easy access to the fish. You never know."

Don lead the way in our boat and as he passed the second island he swung in position for a trolling run and stopped so we could rig up.

"Bud, we'll be fishing the same type of troll as we did yesterday. I'm going to start with Gold and you start will Silver to give us a better chance to see which works best. We can even switch off of these and use a couple different fluorescents if need be."

Don started his slow troll pattern and we were half way down the channel before we had our first strike. Don's strike indicated that Gold may be the color of the day and as I netted the Walleye I asked Don, "Should I switch to Gold."

"Not yet, let's give it a chance. If you don't get a hit by the time we get to the end of the channel you can switch."

He had just gotten that statement out when I got a hard strike and exclaimed, "Fish on!"

"That's the way Bud, bring him into my net!"

Don netted a nice Walleye for me and we looked back to see how Tom and John were doing. John was just netting one for Tom and held up two fingers indicating it was there second fish in the boat.

Don went around the point of the island and had just started into the channel between the two when he got another strike. Amazingly, I also had a strike, so we had another double going for us. Don's fish was closer to the boat and again he was able to net it in time to come over to my side of the boat and net mine.

"Wow Don, two apiece! You were sure right about this spot."

"I have always had great fishing around these two islands and fortunately I'm not disappointed this time. You did well and remembered your lessons, I'm proud of you."

"Well my friend, it's because you're a good teacher of Fishing Skills, hopefully I'm helping you understand Practical Accounting. You know, that's the trade-off."

"I think the light bulb was really coming on last time and with a little refresher now and then I think it will sink in. I really have more confidence and can't wait to apply the principles you have taught me to my new business."

We were able to get off the lake early as we had caught our limit. All four of us caught trophy Walleyes but could keep only one over 18". My trophy Walleye was 22" long and weighed 4 pounds, and the 3 other trophy Walleyes were all in the 20" category. Everyone was happy with their limits of fish, feeling that leaving the lake early would give us more time to share around the dinner table.

"Don, the session this evening will be a review of another report; the Cash Flow Statement. This report will tell the manager where the cash came from and where it went. The Cash Flow Statement gives the manager the historical sequences, for a certain period of time. The cash flow from the Income Statement, Net Profit, and the Current Asset accounts changes, increases or decreases, the Investment activities, like purchases of Fixed Assets, the Financing Activities, the paying down debt or recording new loans from borrowing. The following is an example, and I added it to your journal."

Cash Flows from Operating Activities

Net Income	$29,501	
Current Assets changes	($10,000)	
Depreciation	$10,250	
Cash Flow from Operating Activities		$29,751

Cash Flows from Investing Activities

Purchases of Fixed Assets		($37,500)

Cash Flow from Financing Activities

Short Term Debt Increase	$ 2,000	
Long Term Debt Increase	$20,000	
Cash Flow from Financing		$22,000
Increase or (Decrease) in Cash		$14,251
Beginning Cash Balance		$ 6,599
Ending Cash Balance		$20,850

"Don, this statement shows you where the money came from and where it went. It's a good guide to show you what has happened with Cash within a set period of time and what you will need to plan on for future periods. Cash Flow Questions: Did we make enough Profit to add to the Cash? Did we spend too much on Current Assets (such as increasing Inventories)? Did we spend too much on the purchase of Fixed Assets? Did we pay back enough on our loans to protect us for future borrowing?"

"Wow Bud, this makes total sense!"

"Now Don, I want to give you a summary of the three Financial Statements that we have discussed. I want you to highlight these three statements in your journal as the keys to a better understanding of your Financial Statements."

Balance Sheet – This report that is a snap-shot of the
    Company at one particular point in time.
    Assets (items the company owns)
    Liabilities (debts the company owes)
    Equity (investment in the company)

Income Statement – An operating report covering a specific period of time.
    Revenues (Sales & Services Income)
    Cost of Goods (Costs related to the Sales or Services)
    Expenses (Operating, Selling, & Administrative)
    Net Profit or (Loss)

Cash Flow Statement – A cash report over a period of time
    From Operating Activities
    From Investing Activities
    From Financing Activities

"Don, hopefully this helps you to understand the value of each of the individual reports."

"It definitely does Bud, this is going to be so helpful and I can't wait to see what my reports are really going to show me now."

"Another evening has rushed by Don, and we had better hit the sack or we won't want to get up to fish Hawk Lake."

"I'm not worrying about that Bud, when the bell rings you and I will be there.

7 Hawk Lake – Day 5

Cliff had assigned us to his boats on Hawk Lake, advising us that since this is a conservation project we would be limited to bring back only Walleyes 18" or less – no trophy fish at this time. He gave us a map for each boat with the hot spots highlighted. As I shared before, Cliff is a great resort manager as he likes to mix our experiences to not only the different lakes where he has boats, but making sure we have updated maps with all of the current hot spots marked. He made notes on the Hawk Lake map that it's a dark water lake, therefore suggested using a silver or bright fluorescent spinner as they seem to pick up the light the best.

Also, Hawk Lake is actually two lakes combined. You needed to rack the boats at the end of Hawk #1, taking the boats on the Hawk #2 racks for use there. Its extra work as it is necessary to transport all your gear and the gas tanks from the Hawk #1 boats over to the Hawk #2 boats. Cliff emphasized that these are two developing lakes and he's trying to build the size of the Walleye through a conservation requirement of no trophy fish taken home. You can still experience the thrill of catching a big trophy fish but he requested everyone fishing these lakes would release the trophies back into the lake.

We picked up the two gas tanks and the minnows and headed out to Hawk Lakes. The cutoff to Hawk wasn't far from Cobblestone but in the opposite direction than Ignace. Even though the cutoff was close, the access road to Hawk seemed to take longer than the road to Indian from Ignace. We arrived at Hawk Lake and were surprised, even though Cliff had told us how dark the water really was. Don and I would be fishing together in Hawk #1 and I would fish with Tom in Hawk #2, giving Don and John a chance to fish together. As Cliff had told us, Hawk Lake was really a dark water lake.

We moved both boats off of the racks with no problem and pulled them up close enough to load everything we needed for the day. We had brought our lunches today to make it easier. Don took off steering our boat toward the 1st place that Cliff had marked, which was relatively close.

He stopped the boat and said, "Bud, I'm going to suggest that we stick with the metal colors because this is such a dark lake. We need a spinner that will capture as much light as possible. I'll start with gold and you start with silver, and will switch to the one that gets the most hits after several passes."

"Is this considered *Fishing Skills* for **dark water** lakes, Don?"

"You got it Bud, I'm glad there are no clouds today. The bright sunlight will penetrate deeper in this dark water."

Don started with a back trolling method to slow the boat down, giving our spinners an opportunity to pick up as much of the light as possible.

I noticed Tom and John were not too far behind us and were preparing to make the same sweep through this first area. I again watched exactly how Don was handling his line and tried my best to duplicate it. I did notice that periodically Don would slightly flip the tip of his rod to get the most action possible out of the spinner. I started to duplicate that method and felt my first hit. I let out just a bit more line and the fish hit harder so I set my hook and started reeling it in.

Don saw what was happening and gently said, "You're doing fine Bud, just keep your rod tip up and reel the fish toward the boat. Try not to let it break the surface too quickly. I'll be standing by with the net, and when the fish gets close enough to the boat I'll net it."

A Fish Tale

"It feels like a nice fish Don, but what do I know, they all feel nice to me."

"Just bring it in as close as you can to the boat, I'm ready with the net." I could see that the fish was close and Don cleanly netted it and said, "Way to go Bud, we've got our first Walleye on Hawk #1!"

"Thanks Don! You swooped that baby out of the water clean as a whistle!"

"Well, our first catch was with your silver spinner Bud, but I'll stick with my gold for another pass."

We started down the same line and close to the spot where I caught our first Walleye Don got a good hit! I reeled in so I could help him by netting his fish. It was fun watching how easy he made it seem, and before you knew it, I had his Walleye in the net.

"Way to go Don for Walleye #2, yours seems bigger than mine, maybe it's our first trophy!"

"I know it's over 18" Bud, we'll measure it, take a picture, and let him go back to grow a bit more."

Don's Walleye was 22" long and with his small scale it registered 4# so I took a picture of Don holding his fish before he let it slip back into the lake. My fish was just a freckle under 18" so we were able to put it on the stringer to take back to Cobblestone.

We noticed that Tom and John had both caught fish with one going back and one put on the stringer. There is a limit of six Walleye and six Northern per license.

We continued the same sweep along the first spot Cliff had marked and ended up putting a couple more Walleye for each of us on our stringer. After picking up a total of eight Walleyes Don thought we should move on to the next spot Cliff had marked on the map of Hawk #1. When we reached the second spot, Don immediately liked the looks of it.

"Bud, get ready for some action because I really like the layout of this spot! We'll be passing by several points and when we do, be ready for some good strikes!"

"Will do Don!"

Boy was Don right! We had a double when we passed the first point with Don netting his by himself, and leaving it in the bottom of the boat, he came over to net mine! Fortunately, both were within the 18" length, so quickly we had two more on our stringer! We were now at ten Walleye and when we caught two more we would need to start sorting out the smaller ones closer to our 18" maximum. By the time we went by the next point Don and I both had doubles again! Don quickly brought his in, netting it and leaving it in the bottom of the boat in order to net mine. Don's Walleye was right at 18" long and mine looked like a twin. Don put them on the stringer and had me hold up the entire stringer for a picture.

"How neat is this Don?"

"I know! We have our limit already and haven't even got over to Hawk #2."

Don pulled our boat over to where Tom and John were and asked, "Well guys, we are at our limit of Walleye, let two trophy fish go back in the lake, and we're ready for lunch, how about you?"

Tom laughed and said, "We also have our limit of Walleye and John caught a nice Northern, so we're one up on you guys."

John added, "We've had a ball and are certainly ready for lunch! Let's find a quite cove and enjoy a lunch on the lake."

I chimed in, "Sounds good to me, lead the way and we'll follow."

The guys found a quiet cove and we were able to beach our boats against a large rock so that we could just sit still in the boats and enjoy our lunch.

Don decided to try his luck casting a large yellow floater with an orange belly, looking for Northerns seeking something to eat in this sheltered water cove. His cast took the floater out toward some reeds on the shore line, and he started flipping it while slowly reeling it in. Within seconds, it seemed, a big Northern hit the floater so hard it flipped up in the air! The second hit resulted in a catch for Don! I watched this action carefully, knowing I was receiving another Fishing Skills Tip!

I was amazed at how hard that Northern had popped that floater out of the water! The fish was putting up a good fight but it was also a display of Don's skills as he reeled the Northern closer to the boat. The Northern didn't like that, and zing, the line went out again as the fish was trying his best to get away! Don just kept playing the fish by steadily reeling it toward the boat after each attempt to get away from him. I had the net ready and after one last try the Northern appeared to be playing out while Don was getting it closer to the boat. I netted the fish for Don and everyone cheered!

"Wow Don that was some fight!"

"It was a good fight Bud, but I knew if I kept my rod tip up and continued to reel steadily I would eventually wear him out!"

"You hold him up Don, and I'll take a picture for you."

"Thanks Bud, he is a beauty!"

The Northern was 34" long and Don's scale showed it to be just over 11#. I was amazed and forgot all about my lunch. I wanted to try to catch one here in this cove! Don had an extra floater, a twin to his, and he said I could give it a try. I put the floater on my line after attaching a longer steel leader. I made my cast toward the same reeds, and started the same flipping action that Don had shown me with a slow reeling back to the boat. Again, within seconds, a fish hit the side of that floater and flipped it up in the air! What surprised me was I could see the Northern come out of the water as he hit that big floater. I didn't hook him that time but he came back with vengeance. Just as I felt him hit the floater I pulled my rod sharply up and hooked him. The fight was on! I was reeling the fish back to the boat, keeping my rod tip up, when he took off again toward the reeds. That fish definitely wanted to be free of that hook. I tried to duplicate the way Don had fought his Northern and thankfully, noticed Don was ready with the net. I could tell the fish was tiring out as I was making good progress toward the boat. I saw him come up beside the boat and Don did a great job of swooping that net down and bringing it into the boat!

Don yelled, "Good job Bud, he's about as big as the one I caught! You hold him up, but keep your hands away from his mouth. He would love to latch on to your hand!"

"Thanks Don, I appreciate your help bringing him into the boat!"

A Fish Tale

We measured the Northern and he was 31" long and weighed just over 8 pounds! I was thrilled and recognized that Don had just taught me another Fishing Skills lesson.

I owed him some additional Accounting Tips for both the lesson and his netting job.

Tom and John also pulled in a couple of Northerns and we finally finished our lunch. So far, this was certainly our most interesting lunch. Tom suggested that we try Hawk #2, so we proceeded to the racks for Hawk #2 boats. It was just around the corner from the cove we were in.

We winched our boats up on the racks and transferred everything to the Hawk #2 boats. We didn't have any problems launching our boats and Tom lead the way to the new marked areas. I had loaded my gear in Tom's boat and John loaded his in Don's boat. This would give me the opportunity to fish with Tom and the two brothers to fish together. A win, win, for all.

Tom decided to try the first place Cliff had marked in Hawk #2 as he had said some of the other guests had caught trophies there. I had switched my spinner to gold and Tom was going to fish with silver this first go-around. Being more aware of techniques now I watched how Tom was doing on our first back trolling run. Tom was duplicating what Don had been doing earlier. So, I just stuck with the same routine. When we went by the first point Tom got a big hit and so I reeled in to net the fish for him. Tom had a steady hand and was bringing the fish in closer to the boat, but the fish resisted and pulled some line back out. Again, Tom was making good progress and this time I prepared to net his fish as soon as he got it close enough to the boat. I swooped the net down and brought Tom's catch into the boat. I knew immediately it was a trophy! Tom held it up and I took a picture of his great catch.

Tom's Walleye was 29" long and weighed 9 pounds, a very nice trophy returned to this dark Hawk Lake #2.

It appeared that Don and John just got a double and so we waited until they were able to net them. Don yelled over to us, "John caught another trophy that was 23" long and weighed close to 5 pounds. We took a picture and gently let him swim away. My Walleye was right on 18" so I released one of the shorter Walleye to keep us legal."

We both yelled over our congrats, and Don said, "We've had a great day guys why don't we head out, we still have to transfer all the stuff to the Hawk #1 boats and it would be good to get an early start back. We'll need to get things organized for our trip home tomorrow."

It was a quick trip to the boat racks and the transfer of everything went smoothly, so we were headed back to Hawk #1 boat racks in good time. Again, the transfer of everything to Tom's Jeep was a quick one and we were on the road back early afternoon. It was a quicker trip back and Cliff saw us drive up to drop off the gas tanks and came down to the fish cleaning house to help us clean our catch. Cliff was the best at cleaning Northerns and had a knack at taking care of the Y bones. He finished cleaning the Northerns and jumped right in to help clean our nice catch of Walleye. Don and John put several of the smaller Walleyes aside for our dinner tonight, freezing the ones that were right on the 18 inches, giving us our limits to take home.

While Don and John were fixing dinner, Tom opened another bottle of wine. He poured all of us a glass of wine and I set the table for the guys. Tom and I were enjoying our glass of wine when Johnny called us to dinner.

You just can't beat fresh Walleye, baked beans, fried potatoes, and fresh bread. Don told us to enjoy, but to save room for a special dessert that he had made for us. We finished all the Walleye plus the trimmings as Don was bringing over his specialty, Cherry Cobbler. I had to loosen my belt before finishing my cobbler.

~~~

We left Tom and Johnny's cabin and headed over to cabin number 8, and as promised at the previous Accounting session, I wanted Don to see the value in utilizing Management Footprints.

So, to start the session I said, "Don, I want you to read the **Management Footprints** here in your journal and I will explain their importance as we go through each of them."

"Okay Bud, but first let me brew us a pot of tea in order to be alert as we continue."

"That's a good idea because I want you to have a clear head as we go through each Footprint. I have written them out for you in your journal and I'm sure you'll understand their significance as we go."

Principle #3 – Management Footprints

> These Footprints are developed over a period of time through the study of your business' Financial Statements and therefore will flag important items you should be watching.

Footprint #1 – The Rules Footprint

When developing your Accounting System, Chart of Accounts, and Financial Statements, follow the rules, (GAAP) Generally Accepted Accounting Principles. For our purpose we will cover the rules pertaining to historical costs, accrual accounting, chart of accounts and of all financial statements.

Footprint #2 – Historical Costs and Accrual Accounting

Historical Costs, simply are the cost values entered through accounting entries. All Costs are entered at their original value on your books. This gives the accounting records a consistency and eliminates unnecessary adjustments as values change.

Accrual Accounting is the fact that transactions completed may not require cash. This allows credit purchases or sales to be recorded at the moment they occur, and therefore will match current revenue with current expenses.

Footprint #3 – The Chart of Accounts Footprint

The manager's participation in the development or improvement of the chart of accounts will give him a much better handle on the economic operations of his venture. The manager can select key accounts that he wants to glean information from and position them accordingly in the financial statements. As an example, when we establish our Selling Expenses we may want sub accounts for key Selling Expense items.

The manager may want more detail in this area, so he can establish sub accounts as follows: Media Advertising, Promotion Pieces (Flyers, Direct Mail, Business Cards, and Agency costs), and Samples. By utilizing this concept throughout our Financial Statement the manager will be able to track his Sales, Cost of Goods, and Expense Groups at the end of each operating period.

Footprint #4 – The Balance Sheet Numbering System

The rules covering the numbering system for the Balance Sheet accounts gives the manager the quick keys as to the "why" of positioning of accounts.

An example of the Balance Sheet Section is as follows:

Current Assets
- 1000 – Cash on Hand & In Bank
  - 1010 – Cash in Bank – Checking
  - 1020 – Cash in Bank – Savings
  - 1030 – Petty Cash – On Hand
- 1100 – Accounts Receivable
  - 1110 – Accounts Receivable – Customers
  - 1120 – Accounts Receivable - Others
- 1200 – Inventory
  - 1210 – Inventory – Raw Material
  - 1220 – Inventory – Work In Process
  - 1230 – Inventory – Finished Goods
- 1300 – Notes Receivable (short term)
  - 1310 – Notes Receivable - Other
- 1400 – Prepaid Items
  - 1410 – Prepaid Insurance

1420 – Prepaid Advertising & Promotion
1430 – Prepaid – Dues & Subscriptions

Fixed Assets & Other Assets

1500 – Fixed Assets
- 1510 – Buildings
  - 1515 – Accum Depr – Buildings
- 1520 – Production Equipment
  - 1525 – Accum Depr – Prod Equip
- 1530 – Office Equipment
  - 1535 – Accum Depr – Office Equip

1600 – Other Assets
- 1610 – Organization Expense
  - 1615 – Accum Amort – Org Expenses

Current Liabilities

2000 – Accounts Payable
- 2010 – Accounts Payable – Vendors
- 2020 – Accounts Payable - Other

2100 – Notes Payable (short term)
- 2110 – Notes Payable – Bank (ST)
- 2120 – Notes Payable - Other

2200 – Taxes Payable
- 2210 – FICA Taxes Payable
- 2220 – Federal W/H Taxes Payable
- 2230 – State W/H Taxes Payable
- 2240 – Federal Unemploy Taxes Pay
- 2250 – State Unemploy Taxes Pay

2300 – Accrual Accounts
- 2310 – Health Insurance Payable

Long Term Liabilities
    2400 – Notes Payable (long term)
       2410 – Notes Payable – Bank

Equity
    3000 – Equity
       3100 – Owner's Investment
       3200 – Retained Earnings

"Don, what we have covered in Footprint #4 is basically the **Accounting Formula**; **Assets** (1000-1600) = **Liabilities** (2100-2400) + **Owners Equity** (3000). These accounts always balance out each other because of the Double Entry System of recording. Every entry always contains debits on one side and credits on the other."

"Bud, this is a good deal, these footprints will be a great guide as I progress in my understanding of Practical Accounting."

"That's exactly the reason we'll put them in your journal, Don, let's read your list first and then we can review them."

Footprint #5 – The Income Statement Numbering System

    The rules covering the numbering system for the Income Statement accounts gives the manager the quick keys as to the "why" on positioning of accounts. An example of the Income Statement section is as follows:

4000 – Income
- 4010 – Water Filtration Tanks
- 4020 – Diatomaceous Earth Filters
- 4100 – Water Treatment Service

5000 – Cost of Goods Sold
- 5010 – Water Filtration Tanks COG
- 5020 – Diatomaceous Earth Filters COG
- 5100 – Water Treatment Service COG

6000 – Operating Expenses
- 6010 – Operating Salaries
    - 6015 – Payroll Taxes
- 6020 – Utilities
    - 6021 – Electricity
    - 6022 – Gas
    - 6023 – Water
    - 6024 – Cable & Website
- 6030 – Insurance – Contents
- 6040 – Operating Supplies
- 6050 – Equipment Rentals
- 6060 – Equipment Repairs & Maintenance

7000 – Selling Expenses
- 7010 – Salesmen's Salaries
    - 7011 – Payroll Taxes Sales
- 7020 – Advertising
    - 7021 – Media
    - 7022 – Promotion
    - 7023 – Printing
- 7030 – Trip & Show Expenses
    - 7031 – Lodging
    - 7032 – Travel
    - 7033 – Food & Entertainment

8000 – Administrative Expenses
   8010 – Officers' Salaries
      8015 – Payroll Taxes Officers'
   8020 – Office Salaries
      8025 – Payroll Taxes Office
   8030 – Office Supplies
   8040 – Insurance – General Liability
   8050 – Computer Software
   8060 – Office Equipment Repair
   8070 – Interest
   8080 – Bank Charges
9000 – Other Expenses
   9010 – Federal Income Taxes
   9020 – State Income Taxes

Footprint #6 – The Cash Flow Statement Key Footprints

The Cash Flow Statement covers all of the historical information relative to cash for a certain period of time. This historical information covers the Revenue and Asset changes, the Investment activities and the Financing activities within a certain fixed period of time (such as a month, quarter, or year).

1. *Cash Flows from Operating Activities*
   Net Income
   Accounts Receivable (Increases or Decreases)
   Inventory (Increases or Decreases)
   Prepaid Expenses (Increases or Decreases)
   Depreciation Expenses (non-fund expenses)

2. ***Cash Flows from Investing Activities***
   Purchases of Property, Plant & Equipment
3. ***Cash Flows from Financing Activities***
   Long Term borrowing
   Investment entries

Footprint #7 – Balance Sheet Ratios Footprints

The Balance Sheet Ratios can give the manager a guide or comparison to previous periods and to like companies in their industry.

Current Ratio – Mathematical relationship of Current Assets to Current Liabilities

Debt to Equity Ratio & Debt to Total Assets – Mathematical relationship between Long Term Borrowing to Owner's Equity & Debt to Total Assets

Footprint #8 – Income Statement Percentages

The Income Statement percentages reflect the relationship between Total Income to the individual Expense categories. This gives the manager a guide and comparison to previous periods, and to like companies in the same industry. The common percentages to watch are:

Total Income – 100%
Cost of Goods Sold
Gross Profit
Total Operating Expenses
Total Selling Expenses
Total Administrative Expenses
Net Profit

Footprint #9 – Financial Statements (What, Why, & When)

Balance Sheet –
What? – The company owns, owes, & equity
Why? – A snap shot of the company
When? – At one particular point in time

Income Statement –
What? – A company's revenue & expenses
Why? – A company's operational results
When? – A certain period of time

Cash Flow Statement –
What? – A report detailing where the money came from and where it went
Why? – The historical sequences of revenue and asset changes that affect Cash
When? – A certain period of time

Footprint #10 – the T account

The **T** account is simply a quick method of jotting down transactions on a scratch pad to show the detail of the entry before formally recording it.

The **T** account is a tool for a manager to utilize when testing the effect of an entry before officially recording the information.

"Don, I realize we covered a lot tonight but my purpose was to get them down in your journal in order for us to have them all in one place for our review."

"As you were reading them from my journal I was actually understanding where you were coming from and can see how useful it will be to have them in a place where I can review them as a guide."

"That's my whole point Don, Accounting is not *'Rocket Science'* but really is a very logical tool to record the *'Financial History'* of a company. Once you understand the Practical Accounting steps you're on your way to understanding your *'Financial Reports'* and can therefore do a much better job managing your company. Let's call it a night as you have some good material to review now."

8 Heading Home

We were up early getting everything ready to start back to Minneapolis. We had kept things pretty organized so after enjoying our last breakfast at Cobblestone for the year, and cleaning up the dishes, we started loading the Jeep. Our goal was to get on the road early so it wouldn't be so late when we got into Minneapolis.

After getting everything in its place we went up to the lodge to check out and pay our bills. Both Cliff and Denise met us in the lobby with big smiles on their faces as they told us that our stay had been a successful one for us and an enjoyable one for them as well. They welcomed us to come back again next spring as they enjoyed our group, and told us we were the kind-of guests they appreciated the most. It's great to be able to develop friendships like this that you know will be lasting for many years.

We had a safe trip back to Plymouth with Don and I spending most of the time in the back seat reviewing not only the Practical Accounting Principles that I had shared with him on this trip but enjoying re-living the Fishing Skills that he had taught me over this past week. I told Don that I had one more gem of knowledge I had entered in his journal, the **Principle #4 – *Internal Controls*.** I explained, this principle would be one that should be implemented as soon as possible as it's another key to having a successful business. If you consider ***"Internal Controls" – Sensors*** similar to the warning lights on your car's dashboard (such as – Check Engine) you will better understand their purpose. ***Business Warning Lights.***

"Don, I have detailed each **Sensor** with the information that you will need, to establish your **Business Warning Lights**. When you get home, look at each area discussed here and establish the programs necessary to develop each **Sensor**. If you have a problem in setting up the program just give me a call and I'll walk you through the specific area you're having problems with."

"Will do Bud, let's go over each one now."

"Okay Don, here is how I listed them for you!"

Cash Sensors –

When funds (monies) are used to purchase items, or when funds (monies) are received from a customer for Sales or Services; we need to establish; "Internal Control" – Sensors. Such as, splitting cash responsibilities, so that the individual approving the payment for the items purchased has received information from a different individual that noted the total items received and the condition of the items.

Also, splitting responsibilities, so that the individual recording the deposit from the customer is different than the one recording the Sale or Service.

Receiving ticket Sensors –

Establish a policy stating that all receiving tickets must be signed, dated, with the item quantity and quality noted. This is a simple rule for the individual receiving items, whether it is an inventory item, a supply item, or a new piece of equipment. Attaching the receiving ticket to the invoice gives assurances that everything connected to the item received was correct.

A Fish Tale

Inventory Control Sensors –

The Inventory Control Sensor is a safety net around the inventory items. This will more than likely be a computer generated data entry made at the time the inventory was received. This entry will show that on a specific date x numbers of items were received, in good condition, and placed in inventory at location y, by warehouseman z.

Now this doesn't totally assure that the item will not walk out of the warehouse, ending up in an employee's car, but the receiving ticket did show that z signed for the item and put it in location y.

Also, the internal auditing teams can printout the current inventory status report and spot check the items at any time. Individuals on the warehouse team, knowing that the inventory has these "Inventory Control – Sensors" will be more reluctant to take the risk of being caught walking out the door with inventory items. Example – "Pull Tickets" for inventories pulled out of stock for specific use (production, support, or sales) are inventory sensors.

Small businesses need to establish regular times for physical inventories (monthly, quarterly, or annually). They also need to make random, "surprise" physical inventories of key inventory items where the warehousemen have no idea of the timing of this "surprise inventory."

Cash/Accounts Receivable Sensors –

A specific Accounts Receivable Clerk assigned for the Credit Sales data entry; and a separate Cash Receipts Clerk to record the payments received from customers. Finally a different clerk responsible to taking the cash receipts deposit to the bank. Since data entry reports are generated along the way you can see that this "Cash/Accounts Receivable Sensor" protects the money flow, making it more difficult to abscond with the funds.

Payment/Accounts Payable Sensors –

A specific Accounts Payable Clerk assigned to recording invoices received for payment with a separate individual responsible for pulling all invoices and preparing the check for the payment (this same individual will attach all invoices to the checks written and pass the group of checks along for signature). The person or persons with check signing authority will review the invoices to assure that proper documentation is attached indicating the date the items were received, the quantity, and the condition the items were received in.

Payroll Sensors –

A Payroll Clerk will prepare all of the time sheets for the payroll requiring authorized initials by supervisors for overtime and special pay situations. Again, an authorized check-signer will review the payroll attachments to assure that the "Payroll Sensors" are in place. A supervisor will pass out the payroll checks to keep the arm's length control over individuals paid.

A Fish Tale

Fixed Asset Sensors –

Develop a Fixed Assets Worksheet as items are purchased by passing a copy of the Invoice and Receiving Ticket to the individual responsible for its development. If you start this Fixed Asset Worksheet in the beginning it will be a routine thing to do and will give you a valuable data source for computing depreciation and amortization, as well as assuring that Fixed Assets are protected with insurance. Have a separate section on the worksheet for each Fixed Asset Group: Buildings, Machinery & Equipment, Office Furniture & Equipment, and Leasehold Improvements.

The Fixed Asset Worksheet is the listing that tie all fixed assets purchases to the individual Fixed Asset accounts.

Summary of *"Internal Control Sensors"* you should keep in mind as a small business owner.

- If you consider internal control items as *"Internal Control Sensors"* (similar to the sensors you see on your car's dashboard) you will better understand their purpose.
- *"Internal Control Sensors"* help to make sure the business receives all of its income; without any of it being siphoned off by waste, fraud, dishonest employees, or just carelessness.
- It is a good idea to establish and *"Internal Control Sensors"* Manual listing all of the **Policies and Procedures** you have established for each *"Internal Control Sensor."*

- Review your "Internal Control Sensors Manual" with your outside accountant for his input regarding your coverage.
- Once you have your "Internal Control Sensors System" in place you can fine-tune it when obvious weaknesses appear.
- The **Key** to a good ***"Internal Control Sensors System"*** is the ***"Segregation of Duties"*** to assure that one individual doesn't control the individual function from beginning to end.

~~~

When we arrived back in Minneapolis, of course we made promises to keep in touch and would be counting the days until we could re-new our friendships next year when we came back up to Cobblestone for another week of fishing. We dropped Don and his brother John at Don's house and I stayed at Tom's house that night, leaving the next morning for the final leg of my trip back to Lincoln. I had my fish packed in ice and would make sure they would be protected for the big fish fry we would have shortly after returning to Lincoln.

I talked to Don after the dust settled from the trip, mainly to see if he had any problems implementing the last Practical Accounting Principle, **Principle #4 – Internal Controls.** Don made a request that I come back up to Plymouth to assure that he is developing the Practical Accounting Principles properly for Britewater. He offered to hire me as his consultant and requested a proposal of what my consulting costs would be, including the cost for the trip.

I promptly sent him a proposal which included the trip costs advising him that mainly I wanted to make sure he had implemented everything that we had gone over in Canada. I also wanted assurance from him that he had implemented the Internal Controls necessary for safeguarding his Assets and Operational functions.

Don did hire me as his Practical Accounting consultant to help him make changes I had suggested for Britewater. I traveled up to Plymouth and fortunately Don had already utilized many of the "Practical Accounting Principles" suggested by me on that trip when we met in Canada.

Don's Practical Accounting System was a good fit for his software program and met his needs for supplying him all of the Managerial Financial Statements.

I performed a total review of his Financial Statements and taught him the methods he could utilize within his accounting software program to see the activity in any one account.

I promised him that he had total access to me through his emails, tweets, or phone calls with no additional charges for this access.

~~~

After Britewater had been in business for an additional year I visited Don, again as his Practical Accounting Systems consultant. I reviewed his annual set of Financial Statements for Britewater. I was pleased to see how well his "Practical Accounting System" was working in the continuing development of his company.

Britewater's Financial Statements proved he had made the right decision to start his own business. Once he developed his Budget and Follow-up through his monthly Financial Statements he maintained a comfortable profit. Also, the "Internal Controls/Sensors" he had installed assured him of maintaining good control over his financial activities well into the future.

A Fish Tale

Epilogue

The years have passed by since that first Canada Fishing Trip when I met Don Seeman. We ended up fishing together over a thirty year span and had many great experiences.

~~~

Ten years after our last fishing trip together I called Don to tell him my son-in-law, Mike, was taking me back up to Canada to fish the familiar lakes and to stay in our favorite resort, Cobblestone Lodge, and would be passing through Fargo.

He immediately said, "I've moved up to the Detroit Lakes area in Northern Minnesota and can drive over and have dinner with you in Fargo. I'm only an hour and half from Fargo."

"You had told me about your place on the lake Don, and that's why I called. I was hoping we could meet for dinner."

We did meet for dinner in Fargo! It was great meeting with Don again, sharing all of the good times we had over the thirty year span we had fished together, and just getting re-acquainted.

My son-in-law Mike, was all smiles as Don and I reminisced about the good old days at Cobblestone Resort.

Don has closed the main part of his company but still maintains some stock filtration products and takes care of some service situations with some of his favorite customers. He said his **"Practical Accounting System"** is still working well and keeps him well informed as to what is going on with **Britewater** in its reduced capacity.

~~~

Don said to my son-in-law, "Mike, I was so blessed that your father-in-law taught me so much about Practical Accounting, and gave me the confidence to read and understand my company's Financial Statements!"

I chimed in, "Mike, I am the one who was blessed when Don shared so many fishing skills with me over the years we fished together."

Mike just smiled and said, "You both are lucky to have shared your friendships over such a long period of time. Friendships like you two have are not all that common. God Bless both of you for maintaining them!"

~~~

After we finished our reunion dinner in Fargo and were walking out to our cars, we stopped, and gave each other a hug! We both made one last promise! We would stay in touch and maintain our long term friendship for the rest of our lives...

And, just maybe, someday, we will fish together again in Canada, at our favorite resort, Cobblestone Lodge on Raleigh Lake...

Just maybe, someday...

www.ingramcontent.com/pod-product-compliance
Lightning Source LLC
Chambersburg PA
CBHW060355190526
45169CB00002B/613